Praise for *The Law (in Plain Englis*

"This is a book that everyone in the restaurant business and food or beverage industry must have in their library. As a club owner serving both food and beverages for more than fifty years, I feel this book is exactly what you should have, whether you are a seasoned member of the hospitality community or just starting out."

—Darcelle XV a.k.a. Walter Cole,
owner of Darcelle XV Showplace in Portland, Oregon

"This latest update from Leonard Duboff is a must-read for all who are concerned about how recent developments in our world have impacted how we work day to day. This book is written for the nonlegal minds and helps the reader to understand the issues and the actions that are needed in order to be safe in the workplace and create an environment that citizens will want to enter. An excellent resource for all to have."

—Phillip Harris, EdD, AECT executive director

"I have been in the food industry for more than twenty years, and during that time I have encountered a number of legal issues, which have been significant. If I had had a book such as this available during those times, I would have known exactly what to do when problems occurred. I strongly recommend that everyone in the restaurant, food, or beverage industry get this book for their collection."

—Thein Htaike, owner of Orchid Inc. in Union, Kentucky

"As the owner of a Mexican restaurant for twenty-two years, I know firsthand how complex operating a restaurant really is. Just as its title indicates, *The Law (in Plain English)® for Restaurants* gives plain-English advice about good business practices as well as how to avoid some of the most common pitfalls in restaurant operation. This book is an essential reference for anyone in the food and beverage industry."

—Eduardo Marquez, owner of 2 Amigos in Fairview, Oregon

The Law

(in Plain English)®

for

Restaurants

A Guide for the Food and Beverage Industry

Leonard D. DuBoff *and* **Christy A. King**

Attorneys-at-Law

ALLWORTH PRESS
NEW YORK

25 24 23 22 21 5 4 3 2 1

Published by Allworth Press, an imprint of Skyhorse Publishing, Inc. 307 West 36th Street, 11th Floor, New York, NY 10018. Allworth Press® is a registered trademark of Skyhorse Publishing, Inc.®, a Delaware corporation.

www.allworth.com

Cover design by Mary Belibasakis

Library of Congress Cataloging-in-Publication Data is available on file.

Print ISBN: 978-1-62153-774-8
eBook ISBN: 978-1-62153-775-5

Printed in the United States of America

This book is dedicated to my late English professor, Anne Louthan, who taught me to write in plain English; to my mother, Millicent, and my father, Rubin, who provided me with the gift of life and the desire to use that gift effectively; to my mother-in-law, Cumi Elena Crawford, for her faith, trust, and inspiration; and to my wife, Mary Ann, for her enduring love and continuing support.

—Leonard D. DuBoff

To my husband, Bob, because, like a river flows surely to the sea, some things are meant to be.

—Christy A. King

Contents

Preface and Acknowledgments

When I began writing *The Law (in Plain English)®* series more than forty years ago, I was a full-time law professor and practicing lawyer. As an academic, I felt that my mission included providing educational tools for my students. In my role as a practicing attorney, I realized the importance of making material available to nonlawyers so they could better understand the complex legal rules they are required to follow. It was my belief that *The Law (in Plain English)®* series would serve these goals, and over the years, my expectations have been realized.

The books in *The Law (in Plain English)®* series have been used as textbooks to enlighten nonlawyers about the businesses in which they are involved. They have also been used by individuals to educate themselves in connection with their businesses and personal lives.

Over my years as a practicing attorney, I have had the privilege of working with the owners of numerous food- and beverage-based businesses. I have also been privileged to address professional restaurant associations at their annual conventions. I have, through these interactions, learned a great deal more about the industry. It has also become clear that most, if not all, professionals in the food and beverage industry have a strong desire to do their best to comply with the law and continue to update their knowledge in order to enhance their businesses. It is for these reasons that I initially wrote the first edition of this book with the aid of my colleague Christy King, and we are now updating it. The first edition was *The Law in Plain English for Restaurants and Others in the Food Industry*, published in 2006 by Sphinx Publishing.

The experience I have gained in representing restaurants, gourmet food companies, wineries, and others in the food and beverage industries for five decades has enabled me to appreciate the many legal issues that regularly confront those in these industries. It is my hope and desire that the extensive experience that Christy and I have had in working with these professionals will provide you with the "ingredients" for a useful, practical, and understandable book about some of the legal issues that confront you in your business.

It must be emphasized that no book, no matter how well researched and written, can serve as a substitute for the skill of an attorney. The purpose of this volume is to provide you with an opportunity to identify problems so they can be avoided or, if they can't be avoided, to effectively communicate with your attorney about them. By educating yourself about the problems that can and do arise in your unique business, you will be better able to interact with your attorney. This is why a chapter on how to find an attorney is included in this book.

It is virtually impossible for a book such as this to be written without the support, help, and involvement of numerous individuals. Regrettably, it may be impossible to identify all of the people who have contributed to the success of this volume, but it is essential to identify some of the most important. I would, therefore, like to express my sincere thanks to my collaborator, Christy A. King, Esq., for her extraordinary help with this version. She has sacrificed many evenings and weekends to bring this project to fruition.

Christy and I would like to thank John L. Cook, CPA, Hertsel Shadian, Esq., and Greg Rogers, CPA, for their time and expertise in reviewing the tax chapter and Ashkan Najafi, Esq. and Bert P. Krages II, Esq., both registered patent attorneys, for reviewing the patent chapter. We are grateful, too, for the assistance of Robert C. Laskowski, Esq., who reviewed the securities chapter and Richard J. Parker, Esq., who reviewed the collections chapter, as well as for the help of a person who wishes to remain anonymous who was kind enough to review the retirement plans chapter. We are indebted to Tad Crawford and Caroline Russomanno of Skyhorse Publishing and their staff for their help in publishing this volume. Thanks also to our paralegals Francesca Hurd and Abbey Price for their assistance and recommendations.

We would also like to thank Darcelle XV for the very flattering blurb he was kind enough to write. As an experienced club operator who is identified in the *Guinness Book of World Records* and one of the most prominent members of the restaurant community in Portland, Oregon, his endorsement is significant. We are also grateful for the blurbs written by Eduardo Marquez, owner of 2 Amigos Mexican restaurant; Thein Htaike, owner of Orchid Inc., a sushi-bar operator; and Phillip Harris, executive director of the Association for Educational Communications and Technology (AECT).

I am thankful for the skill that my late college English professor Anne Louthan provided me at Hofstra University many years ago, which enabled me to write books such as this in plain English.

I am grateful for the support of my children and grandchildren, particularly my son, Robert, my daughter, Colleen, and her husband, Rudy (another lawyer with this firm), my grandson Brian and his wife Megan, my granddaughter Athena, and my grandsons Grant, Taliek, and Tony.

My late sister, Candace DuBoff Jones, JD, Northwestern School of Law, Lewis & Clark College, 1977; my late father, Rueben R. DuBoff; and my late mother, Millicent Barbara DuBoff all provided me with the inspiration to create works such as this. I'd also like to thank my brother, Michael, a New York attorney, for his recommendations.

I valued my mother-in-law Cumi Elena Crawford's faith, trust, and inspiration, which helped me create this project. I am also thankful for the support of my grandfather Isidore and my grandmother Rose. Finally, I would like to express my sincere gratitude and acknowledge the contribution to this project by my partner in law and in life, Mary Ann Crawford DuBoff. Without her, *The Law (in Plain English)® for Restaurants* would never have become a reality.

—Leonard D. DuBoff
Portland, Oregon 2021

Introduction

When more than fifty years ago I began my law practice in New York, I learned about the restaurant business from the supplier's side. As an attorney who worked on matters for our firm's restaurant supply client, I was provided an opportunity to see how demanding the restaurant business is.

Later, as a law professor specializing in business and intellectual property law, I continued to develop an understanding for the unique aspects of the restaurant business. My practice included representation of many participants in the hospitality industry, from small establishments to larger, more prominent restaurant chains. Indeed, I have been fortunate enough to obtain a lawyer's perspective on much of the industry.

This text is the product of that experience and the suggestions of several well-respected clients who felt there was a need for a book such as this. My collaborator, Christy A. King, and I have worked together on several other books in *The Law (in Plain English)®* series, and this revised edition joins that user-friendly series.

Other books in the series educate and assist craftspeople, writers, gallery owners, collectors, photographers, health-care professionals, high-tech entrepreneurs, nonprofit organizations, publishers, and others involved in small businesses. The series also includes a book on employment law and a workbook for estate planning.

Reviewers have praised our efforts in providing our readers with tools intended to sensitize them to the many legal issues that can and do arise in their chosen specialties and life experiences. It is hoped that this updated volume will continue to provide those in the food and beverage industries with a readable book that aids in identifying frequently encountered legal issues. Armed with this educational tool, you will be better able to communicate with your attorney and avoid a host of legal problems or be in a better position to deal with them if and when they arise.

This book is not intended to replace an attorney; rather, it is designed to inform those in the food and beverage industries so they can more effectively communicate with their attorneys and better insulate themselves from legal problems.

—Leonard D. DuBoff
Portland, Oregon
2021

CHAPTER 1

Organizing Your Business

Everyone in business knows that survival requires careful financial planning, but few fully realize the importance of selecting the legal form best for each particular business. Although small businesses have little need for the sophisticated organizational structures used in large, publicly traded companies, all entrepreneurs must pay taxes and expose themselves to potential liability with every sale they make, so it only makes sense for you to structure your business to address these issues.

Each business has an organizational form best suited to it. When we counsel people on organizing their businesses, we usually adopt a two-step approach. First, we discuss tax and liability issues in order to determine which of the basic legal structures is best. There are only a handful of basic forms: sole proprietorships, partnerships, corporations, limited liability companies (LLCs), and a few hybrids. Once we've decided which of these is most appropriate, we move on to the organizational documents. Corporate bylaws, partnership agreements, and LLC operating agreements define the day-to-day operations of a business and should be tailored to individual situations.

What we offer here is an explanation of the features of each of these kinds of organizations, including their advantages and disadvantages. We'll discuss potential problems, but—since we can't go into a full discussion of the more intricate details—consult an experienced business attorney before deciding to adopt any particular structure. Our purpose is to facilitate your communication with your lawyer and to help you to better understand the options for organizing your food or beverage business.

SOLE PROPRIETORSHIPS

A sole proprietorship is an unincorporated business owned by one person. As a form of business, it is elegant in its simplicity.

Advantages and Disadvantages

Legal requirements are few and simple. Generally, all you need to do is obtain a business license and register the name of the business if you operate it under a name other than your own. There are, however, many financial risks involved in operating your business as a sole proprietor. If you recognize any of these dangers as a real threat, you should consider an alternative form of organization.

If you're the sole proprietor of a business venture, you're personally liable for the debts of the business. This means the property you personally own (such as your home, vehicles, and bank accounts) is at risk. If for any reason your sole proprietorship owes more than it can pay, your creditors can force a sale of most of your personal assets to satisfy the debt, and you might find yourself filing for bankruptcy protection.

For many risks, insurance is available that shifts the loss from you to an insurance company (See Chapter 17, Business Insurance), but there are some risks for which insurance is either unavailable or prohibitively expensive. For instance, insurance isn't generally available to protect against a large rise in the cost or sudden unavailability of ingredients (for example, the sharp spike in coffee bean prices in late 2019). Plus, the cost of some types of liability insurance has become so high that, as a practical matter, they're unavailable to many small businesses. Even if you do have coverage for a particular risk, you might find that a claim against your business is outside the policy's strictly defined scope of coverage or the policy limits.

Formalities

As mentioned above, legal requirements are few. Depending on your locale, you may need to get a business license. Unless the business name contains your legal name (as defined in your state), you'll need to file an "assumed business name" (ABN) application with the appropriate state or county agency, usually either the Secretary of State's office or the county recorder. In addition, you'll need to meet all state, county, and local laws specific to your particular industry. Examples for food and beverage businesses are food-service licenses, liquor licenses, kitchen safety inspections, brewing permits, wine bar licenses, and food-handler permits.

Taxes

A sole proprietor is personally taxed on all profits of the business and can deduct the losses. Of course, the rate of taxation changes with increases in income. Fortunately, there are ways to ease this tax burden.

In Plain English

Maximize your tax savings by establishing an approved IRA or contributing to a retirement plan. You can withdraw the funds at a later date when you might be in a lower tax bracket. (See Chapter 21, Retirement Plans, for a more complete discussion of this subject.)

PARTNERSHIPS AND JOINT VENTURES

A partnership is defined by most state laws as an association of two or more persons to conduct a business for profit as co-owners. A joint venture is a partnership for a limited or specific purpose, rather than one that continues for an indefinite or specified time. If you and a friend agree to jointly cater a wedding and share the profits, you have a joint venture. If you decide to go into the catering business together, you have a partnership.

Advantages and Disadvantages

Advantages of doing business as a partnership may include:

- the pooling of capital;
- the collaboration of skills;
- easier access to credit enhanced by the collective credit rating; and
- a more efficient allocation of labor and resources.

A major disadvantage is that, as with a sole proprietorship, you're personally liable for the debts of the business, even if you're not personally involved in incurring those debts. Each partner is also liable for the negligence of another partner and for the negligent acts of the partnership's employees when a negligent act occurs in the usual course of business. If, for any reason, your partnership owes more than the dollar value of the business, the partnership's creditors can force a sale of most of the partners' personally owned property to satisfy the debt.

This means that if you're getting involved in a partnership, you must be especially cautious in two areas. First, since the involvement of a partner increases your potential liability, choose a responsible partner. Second, adequately insure the partnership to protect both its assets and the personal assets of each partner (though, as discussed above, there are some risks that can't be insured against).

Formalities

No formalities are required to create a general partnership beyond those required for a sole proprietorship (a business license, assumed business name registration, and industry-specific requirements). In fact, in some cases, people have been held to be partners even though they never intended to form a partnership.

If, for example, you lend a friend some money to open a restaurant and your friend agrees to pay you a percentage of the profits, you might be your friend's partner in the eyes of the law even though you're not involved in running the business and never intended to be a partner. This is important, because, as discussed above, each partner is subject to unlimited personal liability for the partnership's debts, so you could be liable for the hospital bills incurred by patrons of your friend's restaurant when they get *E. coli* after an employee accidentally uses the raw-meat knife to chop cucumbers for a salad.

If partners don't have a formal agreement defining the terms of their partnership, such as control of the partnership and distribution of profits, state law dictates the terms, attempting to correspond to the characteristics of a "typical" partnership and the "reasonable" expectations of the partners. The most important of these legally presumed characteristics are:

- no one can become a member of a partnership without the unanimous consent of all partners;
- every member has an equal vote in the management of the partnership regardless of the partner's percentage ownership;
- all partners share equally in the profits and losses of the partnership, no matter how much capital each has contributed;
- a simple majority vote is required for decisions in the ordinary course of business;
- a unanimous vote is required to change the fundamental character of the business; and

- a partnership is terminable at will by any partner (in other words, a partner can withdraw from the partnership at any time, and this withdrawal causes a dissolution of the partnership).

Partners can—and, in most cases, should—make their own agreements regarding the management structure and division of profits that best suit the needs of the individual partners and the particular business. A comprehensive partnership agreement is no simple matter, so you should devote considerable time and care to preparing your partnership agreement. For more information, see Chapter 2, Business Organization Checklists.

In Plain English

Enlist the services of a competent business lawyer. The expense of a lawyer to help you put together an agreement suited to the needs of your partnership is usually well justified by the economic savings recouped in the smooth organization, operation, and (when necessary) dissolution of the partnership.

Taxes

A partnership doesn't have any special tax advantages over a sole proprietorship. All partners pay tax on their share of the profits, and each is entitled to the same proportion of the partnership deductions and credits. Each partner pays tax on the profits whether the profits are distributed to the partners or retained by the partnership. Especially in the case of new partnerships that reinvest profits into the business, this can result in partners paying income tax on money they haven't actually received.

Every partnership must prepare an annual information return for the Internal Revenue Service (IRS) known as Schedule K-1, Form 1065, which the IRS uses to check against the individual returns filed by the partners. This form details each partner's share of income, credits, and deductions. The K-1 is used by the individual partners to prepare their income-tax filings in the same way W-2s are used by employees.

LIMITED PARTNERSHIPS

A limited partnership (LP) is a hybrid containing elements of both general partnerships and corporations. The limited partnership is a convenient form for securing financial backers who want to share in the profits of an enterprise without undue exposure to personal liability.

Advantages and Disadvantages

The law provides limited risk for a "limited partner," but only so long as the limited partner plays *no* active role in the day-to-day management and operation of the business. A limited partner is much like an investor who buys a few shares of stock in a corporation but has no role in running the business.

While a limited partner has limited personal liability, the general partners have *full* personal liability, just like a sole proprietor or a partner in a standard partnership. This means the general partner's personal property can be sold by the LP's creditors to cover the limited partnership's debts. The decision to do business as an LP rather than a limited liability company or corporation should be made only with the advice of a knowledgeable business attorney, since extra steps must be taken to protect each general partner's assets. Limited partners must refrain from becoming involved in the day-to-day operation of the partnership. Otherwise, they might be found to be actively participating in the business and, therefore, general partners with unlimited personal liability.

A limited partnership can be used to attract investors when credit is hard to get or is too expensive. In return for investing, a limited partner receives a designated share of the profits. From the entrepreneur's point of view, this might be an attractive way to fund a business, because the limited partner receives nothing if there are no profits. An entrepreneur who borrows money from a creditor, on the other hand, has to repay the loan regardless of the success or failure of the business.

Another use of a limited partnership is to facilitate reorganization of a general partnership after the death or retirement of a general partner. Raising enough cash to buy out a retiring or deceased partner can jeopardize the business by forcing the remaining partners to liquidate certain partnership assets. A convenient way to avoid such a detrimental liquidation is for the retiree or beneficiary to step into a limited partner status. The retiree or heirs can continue to share in the profits (which, to some extent, flow from the partner's past labor), while protecting personal assets. In the meantime, the remaining partners have an opportunity to restructure partnership funding under more favorable terms.

Formalities

There must be one or more general partners who run the business and one or more limited partners who play a passive role. Appropriate documentation must be filed with the proper state agency. If this documentation isn't filed or is improperly filed, a limited partner could be treated as a general partner and lose the benefit of limited liability. In addition, the partners need to obtain a business license, register their assumed business name, and meet industry-specific requirements.

Taxes

LPs are taxed like traditional partnerships (see above).

In Plain English

Written contracts can avoid unintended partnerships between businesses and individuals. If you don't have a well-drafted written agreement describing the intended relationship, a court might decide that you and the other party are legally partners.

CORPORATIONS

The word *corporation* may call to mind a large company with hundreds or thousands of employees. In fact, the vast majority of corporations in the United States are small and moderate-sized companies.

Advantages and Disadvantages

When describing the advantages and disadvantages of the corporate form, it's useful to compare it to a partnership. Some significant differences between the two structures include the liability of its owners and the rules relating to the continuity of the entity's existence, transferability of ownership, management, and control, and the methods for raising additional capital. See the Taxes section below for tax-related advantages and disadvantages.

1. Liability

The owners of a corporation aren't personally liable for the corporation's debts—they stand to lose only their investments. Unlike limited partners, shareholders are allowed to fully participate in the control of the corporation through their voting privileges—the higher the percentage of outstanding shares owned, the more significant the control.

For a small corporation, however, limited liability is something of an illusion. Very often creditors require owners to personally cosign for any credit extended, including credit cards. In addition, individuals remain responsible for their own wrongful acts. A shareholder who negligently causes an injury while engaged in corporate business has not only subjected the corporation to liability, but also remains personally liable. If the other party to a contract with the corporation has agreed to look only to the corporation for responsibility, the corporate liability shield does protect a shareholder from liability for breach of contract.

The corporate shield also offers protection when an agent hired by the corporation has committed a wrongful act while working for the corporation. For instance, if a pizza delivery driver negligently injures a pedestrian while delivering a pizza, the driver will definitely be liable and the corporation might be liable, but the shareholder probably won't be.

2. Continuity of Existence

Another difference between a corporation and a partnership relates to continuity of existence. Many of the events that can cause the dissolution of a partnership don't have the same effect on a corporation. In fact, it's common for a corporation to have perpetual existence. Shareholders, unlike partners, can't decide to withdraw and demand a return of capital from the corporation—all they can do is sell their stock.

In Plain English

This continuity can be a tremendous disadvantage to shareholders (or their heirs) if they want to sell stock when there are no buyers for it, though shareholders can enter into "buy-sell agreements" that require the corporation to buy back shares from the estate of a shareholder who dies or withdraws.

3. Transferability of Ownership

The third difference relates to transferability of ownership. No one can become a partner without the unanimous consent of the other partners, unless otherwise agreed, but in a corporation, shareholders can generally sell all or any number of their shares without restriction. If, however, the owners of a small corporation don't want it to be open to outside ownership, they can restrict transferability by agreement of the shareholders.

4. Management and Control

The fourth difference is in the structure of management and control. Owners of common stock are given a vote in proportion to their ownership in the corporation. Other kinds of stock can be created, with or without voting rights. Voting shareholders vote to elect a board of directors and to create rules under which the board will operate.

The basic rules of the corporation are stated in its articles of incorporation, which are filed with the state. These serve as the constitution for the corporation and can be amended by shareholder vote. More detailed operational rules—bylaws—should also be prepared. Both shareholders and directors may have the power to create or amend bylaws. This varies from state to state and may be determined by the shareholders themselves. The board of directors makes operational decisions for the corporation, typically delegating day-to-day control to a president or chief executive officer (CEO).

A shareholder, even one who owns 100 percent of the stock, can't preempt a decision of the board of directors. If the board has exceeded the powers granted it by the articles or bylaws, any shareholder can sue for a court order remedying the situation. If the board is within its powers, the shareholders have no recourse except to remove the board or any board member. In some states, a small corporation can entirely forgo having a board of directors. In these cases, the corporation is authorized to allow the shareholders to vote directly on business decisions, just as in a partnership.

5. Raising Additional Capital

The fifth distinction between partnerships and corporations is the greater variety of means available for raising additional capital. Partnerships can borrow money or, if all the partners agree, they can take on additional partners. A corporation, on the other hand, can issue more stock. In most cases, the issuance of new stock merely requires approval by a majority of the existing shareholders. This stock can be of many different varieties: recallable at a set price, for example, or convertible into another kind of stock.

Preferred stock is often used to attract new investors. The corporation agrees to pay preferred shareholders some predetermined amount, known as a dividend preference, before it pays any dividends to other shareholders. If the corporation goes bankrupt, preferred shareholders are usually paid out of the proceeds of liquidation before the common shareholders, although after the corporation's creditors are paid. Other options include borrowing money on a short-term basis by issuing notes and borrowing for a longer period by issuing debentures or bonds.

In Plain English

Corporations can raise capital by issuing more stock (including preferred stock) or by issuing notes, debentures, or bonds.

Formalities

In addition to obtaining a business license and meeting industry-specific requirements, a corporation must hold initial and annual director and shareholder meetings, adopt bylaws, issue stock to shareholders, and record all stock transfers. A corporation can register an assumed business name if it wants to do business under a name different than its legal corporate name. For example, your company, Pink Hippo, Inc. might want to do business as "Pink Hippo Cupcakes." If so, the corporation must register that name as an assumed business name, since it's not doing business under its full legal name, Pink Hippo, Inc.

Taxes

1. C Corporations

A C Corporation (or C corp) is what most people consider a standard or regular corporation. Under both state and federal laws, the profits of a C corp are taxed to the corporation before they're paid out as dividends. Then, because the dividends constitute income to the shareholders, they're taxed again as the shareholder's personal income. This double taxation is the major disadvantage of conducting business as a C corp.

Avoiding Double Taxation. There are several methods of avoiding double taxation. First, a corporation can plan its business so that it doesn't have much profit. This can be done by drawing off what would be profit in payments to shareholders for a variety of services. For instance, a shareholder can be paid a salary for managing the company, rent for office space leased to the corporation, or interest on a loan made to the corporation. All of these are legal deductions from corporate income.

Deducting Benefits. A C corp can also deduct the cost of various benefits provided for its employees. For example, a corporation can deduct all its payments made for certain qualified employee life insurance plans, while the employees pay no personal income tax on this benefit. Sole proprietors or partnerships, on the other hand, may not be entitled to deduct these expenses.

Retained Earnings. A corporation can reinvest its profits for reasonable business expansion. This undistributed money isn't taxed as income to the shareholders, though the corporation must pay corporate tax on it. By contrast, the retained earnings of a partnership are taxed to the individual partners even though the money isn't distributed to them. For instance, a brewpub is saving up for new fermentation tanks. If the brewpub is a partnership, the partners owe income tax on the profits being saved for those new tanks, but if it's a C Corp, the shareholders won't be taxed on those profits.

Corporate reinvestment has two advantages. First, the business can be built up with money that has been taxed only at the corporate level and on which no individual shareholder needs to pay any tax. Second, within reasonable limits, the corporation can delay the distribution of corporate earnings until, for example, a time of lower personal income of the shareholder and, therefore, lower personal tax rates. If, however, the IRS considers the amount withheld for expansion to be unreasonably high, the corporation may face a penalty, so it's wise to work with an experienced tax planner.

2. S Corporations

Except for tax issues, most of the advantages, disadvantages, and formalities are the same for a "small business corporation" (S corp) as for a C corp. This hybrid organizational form allows the owners of a small corporation to take advantage of many of the benefits described above (including limited liability) while being taxed much like a sole proprietorship or partnership—that is, income and losses flow directly to shareholders, and the corporation pays no income tax.

Unfortunately, the tax rules for "S corps" aren't quite as simple as those for partnerships or individuals. Generally speaking, though, the owners of an S corp are taxed on their pro rata share of the distributable profits and can deduct their share of distributable losses. This form can be particularly advantageous in the early years of a corporation because the owners can deduct almost all the corporate losses from their personal incomes, something C corp shareholders can't do.

The word "small" in "small business corporation" doesn't have anything to do with how much money the business makes. Rather, it refers to the number of owners. To qualify for S status, the corporation can't have more than one hundred owners, each of whom must be a human being or a certain kind of trust or nonprofit corporation. The owners of an S corp can't be nonresident aliens, and there can't be more than one class of voting stock. An S corporation can own stock in another S corporation.

In Plain English

The S corporation is often a desirable form for a business likely to sustain major losses when the shareholders have other sources of income against which they wish to write off those losses.

B CORPORATIONS

The newest form of corporation is the Benefit Corporation (or B corp). Unlike a traditional corporation, a B corporation must be operated to achieve a "public purpose," that is, one that has a material, positive impact on society or the environment but, unlike a nonprofit corporation, a B corp can engage in a business for profit. For example, a restaurant organized as a B corp might be certified as a socially responsible business by complying with certain guidelines regarding the treatment of its employees, the environment, and the community.

Nearly three quarters of the states have enacted laws allowing this type of corporation. Without these laws, shareholders may sue a corporation that focuses more on societal benefits than shareholder profits. These corporations can be taxed as C corps or as S corps, and most of the required formalities are the same, though B corps have additional obligations, usually including adopting a third-party standard and preparing, filing, and distributing an annual benefit report identifying the actions and methods used to provide a public benefit, any circumstances that hindered or prevented a benefit, and how well the B corp met or exceeded the third-party standard.

LIMITED LIABILITY COMPANIES

A limited liability company (LLC) combines the limited liability of a corporation with the tax advantages available to a sole proprietor or partnership. The law in most states allows those conducting business as an LLC to create the most flexible and user-friendly organizational structure. They can elect to have the LLC's business conducted by a manager or by the members (owners) themselves. They may, but aren't required to, have periodic meetings. In fact, the owners can, through the operating agreement (equivalent to a corporation's bylaws), create virtually any organizational structure they desire. LLCs can be taxed as sole proprietorships, partnerships, C corps, or S corps. The default is taxation as sole proprietorships for single-owner LLCs and as partnerships for other LLCs.

By conducting business through an LLC, entrepreneurs can shield their personal assets from claims against the business in all situations except the individual's own wrongful acts. This liability shield is identical to the one offered by the corporate form. LLCs don't have the restrictions imposed on S corporations regarding the number of owners and the type of owners (human beings or specified business forms). In fact, business corporations, partnerships, and other business entities can own interests in LLCs. LLCs can also have more than one class of voting ownership.

In Plain English

Dissolving a corporation or LLC is not only painful because of tax penalties, but it's almost always impossible without the consent of the majority of the owners. Majority owners have ultimate and absolute control unless minority owners take certain precautions from the start. Retain your own attorney to represent you during a business entity's formation, rather than waiting until it's too late.

HYBRIDS

In addition to the business forms previously discussed, many states permit the creation of hybrid forms of business organization, such as limited liability partnerships (LLPs), limited liability limited partnerships (LLLPs), and business trusts. Consult with an experienced business lawyer to determine which business forms are available in your state and which best serve your business objectives.

CHAPTER 2

Business Organization Checklists

As we discussed in the previous chapter, a host of business forms are available to entrepreneurs in food and beverage businesses. Creating any of these business forms is a rather simple process, but to do it right and enjoy all the advantages, we recommend that you consult a competent business lawyer. Of course, a lawyer's time costs money, but you can save some money if you come properly prepared. The following are some of the points you should prepare to discuss with your lawyer.

ACCOUNTANT

Other than yourself, the most important person your attorney will work with is your accountant, who provides valuable input on the business's financial structure, funding, capitalization, allocation of ownership, and other issues. We even consulted with respected accountants to verify the accuracy of the tax information in this book.

BUSINESS NAME

Regardless of its form, every business has a name. Many businesses simply use the last names of the principal owners. The choice in that case is nothing more than the order of the owners' names—which depends on various factors from prestige to the way the names sound in a particular order. If the name of a sole proprietorship or partnership doesn't include the full names of the owners, you'll need to file the proposed business name with the appropriate agency.

Corporations, LLCs, and other entities that are created through filing with the state have their names registered at the same time. They, too, can register assumed business names (also known as ABNs and D/B/As) if they choose to do business under names other than their official business names. For example, if your corporation is named Smith's Purple Hippo Catering Company, Inc., you might want to do business under the name "Purple Hippo." If so, you'd need to register "Purple Hippo" as an assumed business name of Smith's Purple Hippo Catering Company, Inc.

Contact your attorney ahead of time with the proposed name of the business. A quick inquiry to the corporation commissioner or secretary of state establishes whether the name is available. Most corporation division offices have online services that allow you to begin the process yourself. You or your attorney can reserve your chosen business name until you're ready to use it.

The name of your business isn't necessarily the same as your brand. You'll also need to think about whether your business will have a special mark or logo that needs trademark protection (see Chapter 10, Trademarks). Choose a name that's distinctive and not already in use. If the name isn't distinctive, others can use it. If it's already in use, you could be liable for trade name or trademark infringement.

DESCRIPTION OF THE BUSINESS

Before entering into a partnership or creating an entity (e.g., a corporation or LLC), the owners should agree on the basic scope of the business—its requirements for capital and labor, each party's individual contributions of capital and labor, and perhaps some plans regarding future growth.

BUSINESS STRUCTURE

It's also important to decide which business form your operation will adopt, since each available structure has benefits and drawbacks. The forms to consider and their pros and cons are discussed below and in Chapter 1, Organizing Your Business.

Partnerships

If you decide to conduct your business as a partnership (whether as a general partnership, limited partnership, or limited liability partnership), you'll need a formal written partnership agreement prepared by a skilled business attorney. The more time you and your prospective partners spend discussing these details before meeting with a lawyer, the less the meeting is likely to cost you. Following are six basic terms of a partnership agreement that you should consider before meeting with your business lawyer.

1. Capital

After determining how much capital each partner will contribute, the partners must decide when it will be contributed, how to value the property contributed, and whether a partner can contribute or withdraw any property at a later date.

2. Duration

Sometimes partnerships are organized for a fixed amount of time or are automatically dissolved on certain conditions, such as the completion of a catering arrangement.

3. Distribution of Profits

You can make whatever arrangement you want for distribution of profits. Although ordinarily a partner isn't paid wages, you might agree to pay an active partner a salary or hourly wage in addition to a share of the profits. Since the profits can be determined only at the close of a business year, distributions ordinarily aren't made until that time, but it's possible to allow the partners a monthly draw of money against their share of the final profits. In some cases, you may want to allow limited expense accounts.

Not all the profits of the partnership need to be distributed at year's end. Some can be retained for expansion. This arrangement can be provided for in the partnership agreement. Whether or not the profits are distributed, all partners must pay tax on their shares of the profit. The tax code refers directly to the partnership agreement to determine what that share is. If it's not dealt with in the partnership agreement, there's a presumption that partners share profits and losses equally among themselves.

4. Management

Power in a partnership can be divided many ways. All partners can have the same voice, or some may have more than others. A few partners might be allowed to manage the business entirely, with the remaining partners having a vote only on specifically designated issues. Besides voting, three other areas of management should be covered. First is the question of who can sign checks, place orders, or enter into contracts on behalf of the partnership. Generally, under state partnership laws, any partner can do these things so long as they occur in the usual course of business. Such a broad delegation of authority can lead to confusion, so it might be best to delegate this authority more narrowly. Second, it's a good idea to determine a regular date for partnership meetings.

Finally, you should consider the possibility of a disagreement arising among the partners that leads to a deadlock. One way to avoid this is to distribute the voting power so as to make a deadlock impossible. In a two-person partnership, however, this would mean that one partner would be in absolute control, which might be unacceptable to the other partner. If power is divided equally among an even number of partners, as is often the case, the agreement should designate a neutral party or mediator to settle any disputes to avoid a dissolution of the partnership.

5. Prohibited Acts

By law, each partner owes the partnership certain duties. First is the duty of diligence. This means a partner must exercise reasonable care in acting as a partner. Second is a duty of obedience. Partners must obey the rules of the partnership and, most importantly, must not exceed the authority granted them by the partnership. Finally, there is a duty of loyalty. Without approval of the other partners, a partner isn't allowed to compete with the partnership in another business or take an opportunity that would be of value to the partnership.

The partnership agreement should include a list of prohibited acts, elaborating and expanding on these fundamental duties. That agreement might also authorize current or planned activities that would otherwise be prohibited. For example, the owners of a wine-tasting room might agree that the individual partners can operate their own competing wine businesses so long as the wine they make is sold only through grocery and liquor stores and not through tasting rooms or wineshops.

6. Dissolution and Liquidation

A partnership is automatically dissolved upon the death, withdrawal, or expulsion of a partner. Dissolution identifies the legal end of the partnership but doesn't necessarily affect its economic life if the partnership agreement provides for the continuation of the business after a dissolution. Even so, dissolution affects the business, because the partner who withdraws or is expelled, or the estate of a deceased partner, is entitled to a return of the proportionate share of capital that the departing or deceased partner contributed.

Details, such as how this capital will be returned, should be decided before dissolution, since successful negotiation might be impossible at the time of dissolution. One method of handling this is to provide for a return of the capital in cash over a period of time. Some provision should be made so that each of the remaining partners will know how much of a departing partner's interest they can purchase.

After a partner leaves, the partnership may need to be reorganized and recapitalized. Again, work out the provisions in advance if possible. Finally, since it's always possible that the partners will eventually want to liquidate the partnership, it should be decided in advance who will liquidate the assets, which assets will be distributed, and what property, if any, will be returned to its original contributor.

In Plain English

Even if your business isn't earning a lot of money, consider creating a business entity to limit your personal liability.

Corporations and LLCs

There are usually two reasons for doing business through a legal entity like a corporation or LLC: limiting personal liability and minimizing income tax liability. The second reason is generally more applicable to a business that is earning a good deal of money. Following are ten basic issues you should consider before meeting with your attorney to set up your corporation or LLC.

1. Officers and Structure

State statutes typically require a corporation to have some chief operating officer, such as a president or CEO. LLCs can be run either by a manager or by the members (owners) as a whole. In addition, some states may require a secretary or other administrative officers. The corporate bylaws or the LLC's operating agreement should have separate descriptions for specialized officers.

2. Ownership

Questions to ask yourself about ownership include:

- For corporations, how many shares of stock will your corporation be authorized to issue?
- For corporations, how many shares will be issued when the corporation begins operations?
- For corporations, how many shares will be held in reserve for future issuance?
- Will there be separate classes of stock or LLC membership interests?
- For an LLC, what percentage of membership interest will each owner have?
- For corporations, how many shares of the issued stock will each shareholder have?

Ownership of a business can be used to some extent as a means of estate planning or wealth-shifting, so you might want to ask your attorney about updating your estate plan at the same time you incorporate or create an LLC, especially if the business is family-owned.

3. Owner Agreements

Talk to your lawyer about the possibility of creating owner agreements that govern the employment status of key individuals or that commit owners to voting a certain way on specific issues. Ensure that a method has been established to prevent an owners' voting deadlock, especially if ownership is 50/50 between individuals or couples (for instance, you and your spouse each own 25 percent and your brother and his spouse each own 25 percent).

4. Buy-Sell Agreements

The first meeting with your lawyer is a good time to discuss a buy-sell agreement to establish the mechanism for the purchase of stock following the withdrawal, death, incapacity, retirement, divorce, or expulsion of one of the owners. Decide whether the buy-sell agreement should be tied to key-person insurance to fund the purchase of ownership interest by the corporation or LLC in the event of a key owner's death. The agreement can also identify the mechanism for valuing the business—annual appraisal, book value, multiple earnings, arbitration, or some other method—when an owner departs. This may vary based on the reason for the departure. For example, the valuation process might be different for the estate of a deceased shareholder than for an owner who is removed for cause.

5. Planning for Future Owners

If you anticipate bringing in additional owners, you and your attorney should discuss how you can do so. Legal restrictions are imposed on the issuance and sale of additional shares of stock and the sale and transfer of LLC interests, so planning for the future is best done at formation.

6. Capitalization

At this point, your attorney works closely with your accountant. Issues to resolve include:

- the initial capitalization or funding of the corporation or LLC;
- contributions by owners in exchange for their interests (money, past services, equipment, assets of an ongoing business, licensing agreements, or other things);
- whether owners will make loans to the business in addition to their contributions; and
- the value of assets contributed to the business.

7. Governing Board

You must determine how many directors will be on the corporate board of directors or how many managers (if any) there will be for an LLC, as well as who the initial directors and managers will be. You also need to decide whether owners will have the right to elect members of the board based on their percentages of ownership. When an LLC elects to be run by one or more managers, a method for selecting future manager(s) must be specified.

In Plain English

It's a good idea to have an odd number of directors or managers to avoid a voting deadlock.

8. Housekeeping

Your attorney needs to know several other details. For instance, the maximum number of employees the business anticipates for the coming twelve-month period must be stated on the application for a federal taxpayer ID number. You must also decide whether the business's tax year will end on December 31 or on another date (S corps and LLCs that aren't taxable entities must adopt the calendar year) and whether the business accounting method will be on a cash basis or accrual basis. The amount of salaries for its officers or managers (if any) must be authorized. The date for the annual meeting should be set. Selecting a registered agent (generally, your attorney assumes this role) and determining which bank your business will use are all preliminary decisions you'll need to make.

9. Employee Benefits

Be prepared to consider employee benefit plans, such as life and health insurance, retirement plans, and employee ownership programs, as well as other fringe benefits. Even if you don't plan to implement these programs right away, consider whether you might want to plan for these benefits in the future.

10. Tax Treatment

Will your corporation elect to be an S corporation, where income and most losses flow directly to shareholders and the corporation pays no income tax? Or a C corporation, where the corporation pays income tax and shareholders aren't taxed on corporate income? LLCs can elect to be taxed like C corps, S corps, or partnerships (or, in the case of a single-member LLC, as a sole proprietorship). This choice can be made when the entity is first created or when the first year's taxes are filed. Careful consideration must be given to the appropriate tax treatment, and the relevant deadlines, because you may not be able to change your decision later without a significant tax penalty.

If your business is likely to sustain major losses, and shareholders have other sources of income against which they wish to write off those losses, chances are the S election is appropriate. For businesses that don't qualify for treatment as S corporations, an LLC might be the appropriate business form.

CHAPTER 3

Developing Your Business Plan

To establish a viable business, an entrepreneur must determine the business's "personality," what it will sell, who it will compete against, and how it will develop. In addition, every business needs capital at one time or another. The owners might have enough money to fully fund the business themselves, but more often they'll need outside funding. They might seek funding as venture capital or conventional forms of financing (see Chapter 4, Borrowing from Commercial Lenders). Funding might also be obtained through a sale of securities, which is discussed more fully in Chapter 5, Going Public.

No matter what the source of financing, preparing a business plan is a crucial first step. This plan helps a banker, venture capitalist, or prospective owner evaluate your company. Be sure you accurately state everything in your business plan, because any misstatement or omission of a material fact in connection with an investment might violate federal and state securities laws. The structure and content of a business plan varies depending upon numerous factors, including your company's stage of development, the nature of its business, and the type of markets it will serve. Although many different formats are used for business plans and the order of presentation is by no means standard, you should address each of the following topics in your business plan. You may also want to check into the numerous software packages available to help create business plans.

EXECUTIVE SUMMARY

An executive summary provides the reader with a short overview of the key elements of the business plan. Savvy businesspeople are turned away by exaggeration, so the summary must provide an accurate assessment of your business, while distinguishing your product or service and organization from others that are competing in the same market. The summary should describe your management team, emphasizing experience and skills, but also addressing management weaknesses and how you expect to overcome them. Key financial projections and funding requirements to meet those projections should be included. Above all, the summary must be designed to catch the reader's attention. If it fails to do so, the remainder of the plan will probably go unread.

HISTORY AND CURRENT STATUS OF THE BUSINESS

Businesspeople want to know about the past performance of a business before they assess its potential. Toward this end, the business plan should provide a brief history of the business (including when it was founded), subsequent development and growth, how it has been organized (e.g., a sole proprietorship, partnership, corporation, or LLC), and how well its past performance can predict the future.

If you think past performance isn't indicative of your business's potential, describe your reasoning in this section. For example, the COVID-19 pandemic resulted in numerous government shutdowns of and restrictions on many food- and beverage-based businesses. Even when bars and restaurants were allowed to operate at full capacity, most experienced a substantial reduction in business due to people choosing to stay home. Be sure to spell out any negative impacts of the pandemic on your particular business in this section of your business plan.

PRODUCTS AND SERVICES

This section describes your business's products or services in detail. Include a summary explaining any unique features, a statement about performance, and any special services provided (like catering or merchandising of bottled sauces). Present information about the reputation of your services and products, including, for example, favorable reviews from customers and critics. Keep in mind, however, that investors might not have expertise with your business or even familiarity with your industry. Write this section in language that is easily understood by businesspeople without backgrounds in the food and beverage industry.

Virtually every business has some intellectual property since advertisements, marketing materials, and company literature are generally copyrightable; the new equipment you designed may be patentable; names, symbols, and logos are often protectable as trademarks; and techniques, recipes, customer lists, supplier lists, and the like might be trade secrets. Your business plan should describe this intellectual property in detail. Disclose pending applications for copyright, trademark, and patent registrations, which represent potentially valuable assets and demonstrate your intentions to protect your rights. These subjects are discussed more fully in Chapters 9, 10 and 11.

THE MARKET AND YOUR MARKETING PLAN

This section should contain a comprehensive description of the market your business intends to target in term of the industry and your customer. If the product or service you're selling is innovative, such as a little-known wine varietal or a fusion-style restaurant, you may need independent market research to define both the initial and future markets. If comparable businesses have been around for some time, the market has probably already been defined. In that case, you might be able to rely on available data from similar businesses, industry professional associations, the Small Business Administration, chambers of commerce, or the like. Cite any sources of data, and use tables, images, and words created by others only if you have their written permission.

Discuss your desired brand position and how you plan to promote your goods and services to your targeted market. The market description should be more detailed than the product or service description. This shows potential investors that you understand the priority of market over product or service.

In Plain English

For purposes of obtaining investment capital, the market section may be the most important part of your business plan. To the banker, venture capitalist, or prospective owner, a business without a strong understanding of its targeted market is a bad risk, even if its services or products are first-rate.

THE COMPETITION

Identify your competitors, discuss their relative strengths and weaknesses, and indicate the market share likely held by each. Include a forecast of the market share you expect to capture in the first three to five years and the sources from which you expect to draw customers. Be sure to spell out your rationale for each projection—more innovative recipes, creative promotion, marketing, favorable reviews, price, service, or other factors.

As with all projections in the business plan, don't understate the strengths of your competition while overstating your own. Sophisticated businesspeople won't back a company that doesn't have a realistic view of its competition. The discussion in this section should be frank, honest, and as clear as possible, but it shouldn't be defamatory. Truthful statements are never defamatory, so you can easily avoid making defamatory statements by doing your research and sticking to statements you can back up. Defamation can also be avoided by focusing on praising the attributes of your business without trashing your competitors.

SOURCE OF SUPPLIES

Obtaining sought-after products or services at an economical price is key to profit making. This section should discuss the trade shows you attend, detail your suppliers, and identify those with whom you have exclusivity or other agreements. Also, explain your backup plan in the event key ingredients become unavailable.

MANAGEMENT

As a general rule, bankers, venture capitalists, and prospective owners favor investing in a start-up business with first-rate management over an established business with mediocre management. This priority should be reflected in your business plan. In this section, emphasize the experience of each key management executive. Include job descriptions and salaries. Provide résumés detailing each executive's past business experience, education, publications, and any other information that will indicate to potential financiers that you have a qualified management team. If your current management team has weak spots, define them and explain how you'll overcome them.

It's a good idea for your business to have well-drafted employment contracts with all of its employees, but this is especially important for the management team. A management employment contract might also provide members of the management team with economic incentives to provide additional benefits for success. If any member of your management team has an unproven track record, a well-drafted incentive program may persuade investors to overlook some inexperience.

FINANCIAL DATA AND PLAN

Superior products or services and top-flight management count for nothing if your financial projections don't allow for a substantial return on investment. Consequently, this section is the bottom line of your business plan. Begin by summarizing previous financial performance. If your business is new, ensure that all financial projections are realistic and justifiable. Most prospective investors and lenders will check out other comparable businesses, so if your projections deviate widely from the industry norm, you'll lose credibility and jeopardize the financing you're requesting.

In Plain English

Don't inundate your potential investor with yards of spreadsheets. Your financial data should be concise and easy to understand.

Finally, your financial section should discuss the financing itself. Indicate how much money your business needs, the form of financing you're looking for, and how you'll use the money. Most important, discuss the projected return within the next five years of operation. As with all financial information, be realistic and support your projections with solid data and a sound rationale.

THE BUSINESS PLAN TEAM

Developing a well-written business plan forces you to focus your ideas, ferret out weak spots in your organization, and turn abstract concepts into a concrete plan. Experienced lawyers, accountants, and other relevant professionals can provide invaluable assistance in putting together a sound and attractive business plan. Your lawyer can help your business obtain the legal protection it needs while steering you away from the legal pitfalls that face all new or expanding businesses. Your accountant can assist you with the myriad financial assessments you must make. Knowledgeable and respected professionals lend credibility to your numbers and projections. Beyond this, experienced lawyers and accountants sometimes have valuable contacts within the venture capital and banking communities. It's often said that failing to plan is planning to fail.

CHAPTER 4

Borrowing from Commercial Lenders

Commercial loans can be a valuable source of needed capital for qualified business borrowers. Small businesses sometimes seek loans from institutional lenders, such as banks, credit unions, insurance companies, and pension trusts. Unfortunately, institutional lenders other than banks and credit unions rarely deal with small businesses, particularly when the potential borrower doesn't have an extensive track record. For this reason, this chapter focuses on lending by smaller banks and credit unions.

CHOOSING A LENDER

Most institutional lenders follow the same procedures as banks and demand the same type of information, although lending policies vary dramatically from institution to institution. Talk to several lenders to determine which might be likely to lend to your business and which have the most favorable loan terms. While lenders, by nature, are conservative in their lending policies, you might discover some to be more flexible than others. Credit unions and community banks generally have a much higher approval rate of small-business loan applications than do large banks. To save time and increase the chances of loan approval, first approach lenders that are more likely to view your proposal favorably and whose lending criteria you feel you can meet.

Don't limit your search for a loan to your community. A statewide, regional, or even national search might be required before you find the right combination of willing lender and favorable terms. With the Internet, this isn't as difficult as it once was. There's no legal requirement that you borrow money from within your state or that you be registered in the same state as the bank (or other lender) you borrow from. In fact, many lenders don't even have a physical presence in the states where they operate.

In Plain English

Using your credit card as a source of financing isn't a good idea, except in the most extreme cases. Interest rates are high, and the terms are rarely good for business planning. Plus, you have to personally guarantee business credit cards.

After shopping the marketplace and deciding on a particular lender, you'll be ready for the next step—preparing the loan proposal. The importance of being properly prepared before taking this critical step can't be overemphasized. Loan officers aren't likely to be impressed by a hastily prepared application containing vague, incomplete information and unsubstantiated claims. Many loan requests are doomed at this early stage because ill-prepared applicants failed to adequately present themselves and their businesses to the lender, even though the proposed ventures are, in fact, sound. Lenders have a legal duty, called a fiduciary duty, to lend money to applicants who are likely to repay the loan. A well-drafted loan proposal can demonstrate to the loan officer that your business is a good investment.

LOAN PROPOSAL

Knowing the lender's policies and following its procedures are essential. The lender's decision to grant or refuse the loan request will, in large part, be based on your answers to the following questions:

- Is your business creditworthy?
- What do you need the money for?
- Do you need a short- or long-term loan?
- How much money do you really need?

- What kind of collateral do you and your business have to secure the loan?

CREDITWORTHINESS

The ability to obtain money when you need it might be as important to the operation of your business as a good location and delicious recipes. But before an institution agrees to lend you money, the loan officer must be satisfied that you and your business are a good risk—that is, that you are creditworthy. This decision includes several considerations.

GOOD CHARACTER

The lender will want to know what sort of person you are and what your reputation is in the community as well as in the food and beverage industry. The lender will evaluate your past credit history and the likelihood that you'll repay the loan if your business falters or fails. Despite its subjective nature, this character factor often figures prominently in a lender's decision making. It's not uncommon for a loan officer to deny a loan request, irrespective of the applicant's qualifications on paper, if the officer isn't convinced of the borrower's good character.

While character can be considered, certain other characteristics can't legally play a part in the lender's decision. Federal and state laws prevent creditors from discriminating based on race, color, sex, marital status, age (so long as you're old enough to legally contract), national origin, religion, or whether you receive public assistance income. State laws may protect other characteristics as well, including sexual orientation and gender identity. If you believe you've been rejected for a loan on the basis of one of these characteristics, seek the advice of an experienced attorney.

CUSHION

The lender will want to know if you've included a suitable allowance for unexpected business developments in the loan request. That is, does the loan proposal realistically allow for the operation of your business and provide for alternative resources to meet your obligations if your business expectations aren't met?

In Plain English

A lender may consider a loan too risky if you're stretching the limit and leaving no margin for error.

PURPOSE

Be prepared to convince the lender that your proposed use of the borrowed money will generate the additional revenue needed to pay the loan during the agreed repayment period. The purpose of the loan determines whether you should request a long- or short-term loan. The loan's purpose should align with the mission of your business and any purpose stated in your bylaws, operating agreement, or other guiding principles. In the case of benefit corporations and tax-exempt organizations, evaluate the loan's purpose with the help of an experienced attorney, because it might have broader implications for the organization.

TERM OF LOAN

Funding to purchase inventory (for example, ingredients like flour and beef, or supplies like paper napkins and plastic forks) will generally be short-term loans requiring repayment within one year or less. This is because the lender will likely anticipate repayment from the sale of the assets financed by the loan.

Intermediate-term loans, which require payment in between one and five years, and long-term loans, which extend payments over ten or even fifteen years, are more appropriate for purchases of fixed assets like refrigerators, ovens, dishwashers, fermenters, and corking machines. Repayment on the loan is expected to be made not from the sale of these assets, but from the earnings generated by the company's ongoing use of them. Those assets produce income at a much slower rate, so a lender is more willing to allow repayment over a longer period.

Bear in mind that commercial lenders are interested in offering funds to successful businesses in need of additional capital to expand and increase profitability. They're not particularly inclined to make loans to businesses that need the money to pay off existing debts. Depending upon your credit reputation, short-term loans may be available with or without security. It's more likely that long-term loans will require adequate security (which might include securing the asset to be acquired) and a pledge of your personal, as well as your business, assets.

Loans that are characterized as lines of credit provide a business with the opportunity to borrow up to a specified amount at any given time. This can be used to facilitate purchases, help pay salaries when the business is experiencing cash flow problems, or the like. A line of credit is typically available on a long-term basis. Most lenders require the line to be paid off at least once a year, even though the money can be borrowed again immediately thereafter. Certain events might trigger an early payoff or termination of the line of credit, and it's important for you to understand what these terms may mean for your business.

REPAYMENT

When and how the loan will be repaid is closely associated with the questions of how much money is needed and for what purpose. The lender will use judgment and professional experience to assess your business ability and the likelihood of your future success. The lender will want to know whether your proposed use of the borrowed funds justifies the repayment schedule requested, so, as the borrower, you must be able to demonstrate that the cash flow anticipated from the proceeds of the loan will be adequate to meet the repayment terms if the loan is granted. As mentioned above, early repayment might be required if certain events occur.

AMOUNT NEEDED

Lenders are also concerned about the amount of the loan being adequate since an undercapitalized business is more likely to get into financial trouble. Similarly, a lender will be reluctant to approve an excessive loan since the debt service is likely to result in an unnecessarily high cash drain on the business. The loan should net you what you need to accomplish your goal with a slight cushion for error and no more.

Estimating the amount needed to finance building construction, conversion, or expansion—long-term loans—is relatively easy, as is estimating the cost of fixed-asset acquisition. On the other hand, working-capital needs—short-term loans—are more difficult to assess and depend upon the type and location of business. To plan your working capital requirements, you should know the current and anticipated cash flow of your business. This involves a projection of receipts and disbursements at the time they're likely to occur. These figures should be projected monthly to aid the lender in its evaluation. Materially misrepresenting these figures can result in significant liability for your business, so seek advice from experienced advisors.

COLLATERAL

Loans are sometimes made solely on a borrower's signature, but with the exception of smaller lines of credit, lenders typically require collateral to secure loans. The type and amount of collateral necessary in a given situation depends on the particular lender's policies and your financial state. In general, lenders accept the following types of collateral as security for a business loan.

Sureties

You might have to get other people to sign a note in order to bolster your credit. These people—sureties—may cosign your note as endorsers, comakers, or guarantors. While the law makes some subtle distinctions as to when each of these sureties becomes liable for the borrower's debt, in essence, these parties are expected to pay back the borrowed funds if you fail to do so. The lender may or may not require sureties to pledge their own assets as security for their promise to pay upon the borrower's default. This depends, to a great extent, on the surety's own creditworthiness.

Assignment of Leases

Assigning a lease as a form of security is particularly appropriate for franchise situations. If, for example, a bank lends money to a franchisor for a building and takes back a mortgage, that mortgage could be secured by assigning to the lender the lease entered into between the franchisor and the franchisee that occupies the building. If the franchisor fails to meet its mortgage obligations, the lender can have the franchisee's lease payments made directly to it in satisfaction of the franchisor's debt.

Warehouse Receipts

Lenders typically accept commodities as security by lending money on a warehouse receipt. Such a receipt is usually delivered directly to the lender and shows that the merchandise used as security either has been placed in a public warehouse or has left the business's premises under the control of a bonded employee. These loans are generally made only on standard, readily marketable goods.

Security Interests

Equipment loans can be secured by giving the lender a lien on the equipment you are buying. The amount loaned will likely be less than the purchase price. How much less is determined by the present and future market value of the equipment and its rate of depreciation. You'll be expected to adequately insure the equipment, properly maintain it, and protect it from damage. One problem that may arise is that equipment frequently becomes a "fixture" belonging to the landlord (especially in the case of restaurants and similar businesses) and is, therefore, unavailable to secure a loan.

Real Estate Holdings

You might be able to borrow against the equity in your personal real estate holdings, as well as those of the business. Again, you'll likely be required to maintain the property in good condition and carry adequate insurance on the property for the benefit of the lender, at least up to the amount of the loan.

Accounts Receivable

A lender may secure a loan with your business accounts receivable. In effect, the lender is relying on your customers to pay off your obligation.

Savings Accounts and Life Insurance Policies

Sometimes you can get a loan by assigning your savings account to the lender. The lender will flag the account and notify the savings-account holder of the debt to ensure that the account won't be diminished during the term of the loan. The lender will probably limit or prohibit the use of debit cards and withdrawals during the term of the loan. Loans may also be made up to the cash value of a life insurance policy, but you must be prepared to assign the policy over to the lender.

Stocks and Bonds

Stocks and bonds may be accepted as collateral for a loan if they're readily marketable, though lenders typically lend no more than 75 percent of the market value of a high-grade security. If the value of the securities drops below the lender's required margin, you might be asked to provide additional security for the loan.

Inventory

As discussed above, business inventory, either on hand or to be acquired, can be used as security for short-term loans, especially loans used to purchase that inventory. The lender will expect the loan to be repaid from the revenues generated by the sale of this inventory.

Intellectual Property

Patents, copyrights, trademarks, and other forms of intellectual property can be used as collateral for a loan. Unfortunately, many lenders are unfamiliar with methods of valuing the potential worth of intellectual properties and may not be willing to attribute a meaningful value to them. If you plan to pledge your intellectual property as security for a loan, try to obtain an independent appraisal of it.

BUSINESS OUTLOOK

The lender will be evaluating the business outlook for your company in particular, and for your type of business in general (for example, restaurant, brewpub, caterer, or gourmet foods retailer), in light of contemporary economic realities. Part of the evaluation will be whether your proposed use of the loan can reasonably be expected to produce the projected increased revenues for your business. While your proposed plan might appear viable on paper, it may not be realistic given the state of the economy within which your company operates.

FINANCIAL EVIDENCE

Remember that lenders prefer to make loans to solvent, profitable, growing enterprises. They want assurance that a loan will contribute to that growth, since your repayment ability is directly related to your business success. As noted previously, lenders are rarely interested in lending money so that a business can pay off already existing loans.

To help a lender understand the financial health of your business, you'll probably be asked to provide specific financial data. Two basic financial documents are customarily submitted for this purpose—the business's balance sheet and its profit-and-loss statement. The balance sheet helps a lender evaluate your business's viability, while the profit-and-loss statement summarizes your business's current performance. Unless yours is a new venture, plan to submit these financial reports for at least the past two or three years, since they're the principal means for measuring your company's stability and growth potential. Ideally, an independent accountant will have prepared these statements.

ANALYZING YOUR BUSINESS'S POTENTIAL

When interviewing loan applicants and studying the financial records of their businesses, lenders are especially interested in the following facts and figures.

General Information

A lender will want to know about the current condition of your business accounts payable and notes payable. If you're not able to meet existing debts now, the lender will be hard-pressed to understand how you expect to meet additional obligations. Perhaps the requested funds will solve cash flow problems you now have and increase earnings so that you'll be able to bring past-due accounts current while adequately handling the added debt. In this situation, you might overcome the lender's skepticism by presenting a solid, well-thought-out business plan that clearly demonstrates how the new loan will solve, rather than add to, your business's financial problems.

Additionally, the lender will likely want to know the salaries of the owners, managers, and other company officers to see if they're reasonable. Excessive salaries represent an unacceptable drain on company resources and profits that can adversely affect your business's ability to meet its debt obligations. The lender will also be interested in the size of your workforce to determine whether it seems adequate to maximize your business's potential or excessive compared to other similar businesses.

Be prepared to discuss the adequacy of your company's insurance coverage, whether all taxes are current, and, if your business sells a product, the size, if any, of your order backlog. For services, your business's reputation is particularly relevant. Existing business contracts will likely also be evaluated. A prospective lender will be interested in your source of supplies, whether you have an adequate inventory of supplies on hand, and your alternatives in the event your primary supplier is unable to meet your needs.

If your business involves the sale of goods (for example, your restaurant sells bottles of its house salad dressing or your brewpub sells bottles of its beer), the lender will need to know the state of the current inventory. Is it in current and in good shape, or will it have to be marked down to sell it? Lenders are interested in unpledged inventory as a possible source of collateral and also as a source of future revenues. They may also be interested in the inventory turnover rate, which reflects the demand for your product and aids in evaluating the accuracy of your revenue projections.

Since many food and beverage businesses rely on bookings, lenders will want to know how far out and how extensive your bookings are. Is your restaurant booked for the holiday season? Is your catering business busy all summer? Will your business be participating in local food festivals? All these factors say something about the financial state of your business. Although a lender might inquire into other areas, a borrower who knows the type of general information of interest to a lender and can present it articulately greatly increases the chances of having the loan approved.

Fixed Assets

Since fixed assets can be used to secure the loan, the lender will probably be interested in the type, condition, age, and current market value of your company's equipment, machinery, and other hard assets. Be prepared to explain how these assets have been depreciated, their useful life expectancy, and whether they've been previously mortgaged or pledged as collateral to another lender. In addition, be ready to discuss any need or plans to acquire fixed assets. This could mean additional debt obligations in the near future, or it could explain and justify your projected growth.

In Plain English

Lenders are reluctant to lend money to companies with haphazardly kept records. Make sure yours are up-to-date, accurate, and in good condition.

Options for Owners of New Businesses

The preceding analysis applies primarily to loan requests made by established, proven businesses. New-business loan applicants probably won't be able to supply much of the information described earlier. While this won't necessarily keep you from obtaining a loan, it could make its approval more difficult. New-business loans constitute only about 5 percent of all business loans made.

The Small Business Administration has found that approximately half of small businesses fail within the first five years, and many believe the oft-cited statistic that 90 percent of restaurants fail in the first year. A 2014 study found that only 17 percent of restaurants in the western United States failed in their first year, but because not all lenders are aware that the high rate of restaurant failure is apocryphal, you may need to educate lenders about the actual failure rates in your community.

This reluctance to finance unproven businesses, understandably frustrating to new-business owners, is consistent with the traditionally conservative nature of banks and other commercial lenders. In light of the extraordinarily high failure rate of new businesses, compounded by the fact that a new business generally can't provide adequate financial data to evaluate its potential for success, lenders are hard-pressed to justify high-risk loans. Even when a new-business borrower offers more than adequate collateral to secure the loan, the request might be denied.

Lenders are comfortable lending money and earning profits from the interest charged on their loans. They are not comfortable in the role of an involuntary partner in the failing business of a delinquent debtor. Although lenders secure loans with a wide range of collateral, they understandably aren't anxious to foreclose on that security. They're not in the business of selling mash tuns, bread proofers, commercial grills, or grape crushers (much less perishable ingredients such as eggs or fresh hops), or of trying to collect a delinquent debtor's accounts receivable.

Lenders try to protect themselves by lending only a fraction of the collateral's market value, but they still may be unable to obtain the full amount they're owed in a distress sale of the collateral, since this type of sale traditionally attracts bargain-hunters who often buy only at prices well below true market value. With an understanding of these dynamics, the owner of a new business-loan applicant can better appreciate a lender's hesitation to approve the loan.

Nonetheless, commercial lenders do make some loans to new businesses. An entrepreneur needs to demonstrate a good reputation for paying debts and to offer evidence of business management skills. Perhaps you have firsthand knowledge and expertise in the type of business you propose to establish as a result of having previously been employed in the same or a closely related field. For example, if you previously managed a taproom and now plan to open a restaurant, focus on the similarities between the two types of businesses.

In addition, provide a sound business plan to support your projections (see Chapter 3, Developing Your Business Plan). You can further improve your chances of obtaining a loan if you've invested your own money in the business, showing your confidence in its success. If possible, show that your business has a good debt-to-equity ratio and that it's not saddled with an inordinately high debt. Even if your loan application is initially refused, try to establish a good working relationship with the lender. Any initial business success will impress upon the lender the soundness of your plan, helping to open the door for future financing if the need arises.

APPLICATION

Having targeted the source for funds and analyzed your business in terms you now know lenders focus on, you're ready to develop your loan request. Although most lenders require the application to include the same standard essential information, the application's format often differs. Some lenders provide suggested formats; others require a specific format.

The content, length, and formality depend on the lender's familiarity with your business, the amount of money requested, and the proposed use of the borrowed funds. A simple application form and a conversation may be adequate for the local banker you've worked with for years. A start-up business seeking substantial funds from lenders unfamiliar with its owners will be required to provide much more extensive documentation, including a detailed plan of the entire business. A business loan applicant is typically asked to submit any or all of the following information.

- Personal financial statements. These indicate the applicant's personal net worth, which is helpful in evaluating creditworthiness, revealing potential sources of collateral, and estimating repayment capabilities.

- Recent and current tax filings for the business and its owners, usually for the last three years, if available.
- Business financial statements, ideally going back at least two years and prepared and authenticated by an independent accountant. The lender might also request cash flow statements and profit projections.
- Business history, including past profit or loss patterns, current debt-to-equity ratio, current and projected cash flow, and present and projected future earnings.
- Business plan, explaining the proposed use of the requested funds and how the loan will benefit the business (see Chapter 3, Developing Your Business Plan).

Other documentation may also be requested. Each lender will let you know what it needs in light of its policies and your particular circumstances.

In Plain English

Even if you're not currently planning to pursue a loan application, it's wise to keep the necessary information and documents in good order in case you unexpectedly need a loan. Many small businesses were unable to quickly gather their application materials for emergency loans offered during the COVID-19 pandemic, such as the Paycheck Protection Program (PPP), resulting in delayed receipt—or even a loss—of funding.

LENDER'S RULES AND LIMITATIONS

Once your loan has been approved in principle, the lender will probably impose restrictions on your business. These serve to protect the lender against unnecessary risk. You and your attorney, accountant, and business advisor should evaluate all the terms and conditions of the loan to determine whether they're acceptable. If the restrictions are too onerous, decline the loan and seek alternative financing. Never agree to restrictions you can't realistically adhere to. On the other hand, if the terms are demanding but reasonable, it might be appropriate to take the loan. In fact, some borrowers view these limitations as an opportunity for improving their own management techniques and business profitability.

The kinds of limitations imposed depend, to a great extent, on the company itself. If your business is a good risk, only minimum limitations need be set. Expect greater limitations if your company is a poor risk. A frequent restriction for food and beverage related businesses is that they must maintain an A grade for health and safety. Three other common types of limitations you're likely to encounter are repayment terms, use of pledged security, and periodic reporting.

Repayment Terms

The lender will want to set a loan-repayment schedule that accurately reflects your ability to earn revenues sufficient to meet the proposed obligation. Risky businesses can expect shorter terms, while proven enterprises might receive longer repayment periods.

Use of Pledged Security

Once a lender agrees to accept collateral to secure a loan, it will understandably be keenly interested in assuring that, if the need arises, the collateral will be available to satisfy the debt. To this end, the lender may take actual possession of the collateral if it is stocks, bonds, or other negotiable instruments. A lender isn't likely to take physical possession of your inventory or fixed assets, but there are other ways a lender can protect its rights in your assets while allowing you to use them.

For example, the lender could "perfect" its "security interest" in the assets serving as collateral for the loan. A perfected security interest is legally enforceable against other creditors, as well as the bankruptcy trustee if you file for bankruptcy protection. A lender perfects its interest by filing a financing statement in the appropriate state or county office. With intellectual property, the lender may also file with the appropriate federal or state agency. The lender might also impose restrictions on your use of the collateral, require you to properly maintain and adequately insure it, and prohibit you from pledging the same collateral for any other business debts or loans.

While this sounds reasonable, these restrictions can seriously hamper your ability to borrow additional funds if the need arises. For instance, when inventory is used as collateral, you must find out exactly how much of your inventory is involved. A lender may ask for only a percentage of the total inventory to secure the loan. More likely, the security interest will extend to the company's entire inventory on hand at any given time, as well as any later-acquired inventory. The problem is that even if your inventory's value far exceeds the amount of the loan that it secures, you might find yourself unable to use any of the inventory as collateral for additional loans. In situations where this problem is likely to arise, you should consider alternative types of collateral.

Periodic Reporting

To protect itself, a lender might require you to supply it with financial statements on a regular basis—perhaps quarterly or even monthly. From these, the lender can see if your business is performing up to the expectations described in the loan application. This type of oversight serves not only to reassure the lender that the loan will be repaid, but also to identify and help solve problems early on before they become insurmountable and threaten your business's viability.

DETAILS OF THE AGREEMENT

A loan agreement is a contract between the lender and the borrower that spells out in detail all the terms and conditions of the loan. The restrictions are often in a section entitled "Covenants." Negative covenants are things that you can't do without the lender's prior approval, like incurring additional debt or pledging the loan's collateral or other business assets to another lender as collateral for a second loan. On the other hand, positive covenants are things that you must do, like carry adequate insurance, provide specified financial reports, and repay the loan according to the terms of the loan agreement. Remember that you can negotiate the loan terms with the lender before signing. True, the lender is in the superior position, but legitimate lenders are usually happy to cooperate with qualified borrowers making reasonable requests.

COMMUNICATION WHEN PROBLEMS ARISE

Once your loan is approved and disbursed, you have to address a new set of obligations and liabilities. Of course, if all goes according to plan, your business prospers, you repay the loan on schedule, and everyone lives happily ever after. However, the business world is fraught with uncertainty, and your business may flounder through no fault of your own. Think, for example, of all the events canceled and businesses temporarily closed due to the COVID-19 pandemic. If your business falters and revenues tumble, you might not be able to meet your financial obligations. In this unfortunate event, view the lender as a potential ally in solving problems rather than as your adversary.

Commercial lenders aren't eager to exercise their right to foreclose on the collateral securing the loan at the first indication that the debt might not be repaid. They likely have no experience in marketing the types of collateral involved; nor do they want to run a distress sale, which would probably bring in only a fraction of the money owed. Plus, foreclosing further decreases the lender's chance of recovering any of the unpaid balance, since the borrower, having been stripped of the means to carry on the business, is likely to be insolvent and facing bankruptcy. Even if the lender liquidates the collateral at its current fair market value, that value may be much less than it was when the loan was made. For these and other reasons, commercial lenders typically foreclose on collateral only as a last resort.

In general, lenders prefer to work with a potentially defaulting debtor to help ease the debt burden so the borrower can overcome the problems, stay in business, and reestablish the enterprise's profitability. To this end, lenders, through their experiences, have learned to identify a variety of red flags as indications that the debtor is experiencing financial difficulty. For instance, the alert is sounded when loan payments start to be made later and later each month, or when the business account increasingly shows checks being dishonored for insufficient funds.

When a lender sees these signals, it might assign your account to a department that assists borrowers in overcoming problems. The lender may offer a variety of accommodations to help you. For example, it might extend repayment terms, temporarily reduce the monthly payment, or accept interest-only payments until the business has overcome its difficulties. The lender may even offer advice for ways to help solve your business's problems, particularly if poor management is the source of the difficulties.

How far and to what extent the lender is willing to accommodate a delinquent debtor frequently depends on the attitude and degree of cooperation from the debtor. Hard-pressed debtors often fail to understand the importance of establishing a cooperative, rather than an adversarial, relationship with the lender. At the first sign of trouble, take the initiative to notify the lender and explain what you're doing to remedy the situation. Expecting a commercial lender to be sympathetic to your plight and make concessions seems unreasonable in cases where the borrower has waited until the debt is long past due before asking for help. Additionally, a lender isn't likely to be too sympathetic toward a borrower who fails to return calls and is always unavailable to discuss the problem.

A favorably impressed lender can be an invaluable asset to your business, not only in granting loans but also in helping you out in difficult times. Don't underestimate the need for establishing a solid, professional relationship with your lender. The ultimate success and growth of your business may well depend on it.

VENTURE CAPITAL

While some entrepreneurs are able to attract venture capital, this is uncommon for most small businesses. Venture capitalists typically expect a potential investment return of between four to six times their risk capital within a comparatively short period of time, as well as some form of ownership position in the borrower's business. It's been said that the golden rule in dealing with venture capitalists is "The one who has the gold is the one who makes the rules," so it's essential to work with an experienced business lawyer when dealing with venture capitalists.

CHAPTER 5

Going Public

At some point, you might decide to try to obtain capital from investors rather than borrow from lenders. Each year, many private businesses go public. According to Audit Analytics, in 2019 there were 231 US initial public offerings (IPOs), which raised over $63 billion in funds. The percentage of "small" IPOs (with less than $50 million in annual revenue at the time of the IPO) has, however, declined significantly since the dotcom bubble burst, and an increasing number of public companies are going private. It's worthwhile to look at the pros and cons of going public and some of the factors you should consider before making this decision.

ADVANTAGES OF GOING PUBLIC

Issuing stock has the advantage of raising capital without obligating the business to repay loans. The additional capital allows for continued growth, even when earnings and bank loans are insufficient to meet expansion objectives. Also, a successful public offering can improve net worth and debt-to-equity ratio, increasing credibility and financing leverage with lenders.

Public offerings also enhance a company's prestige by increasing its visibility within the business community. The prestige of going public can be an effective device for attracting top-rate management executives. In turn, a strong management team is often the key to both increasing profitability and attracting new investors. In fact, during the growth of the high-tech industry bubble, stock options were essential for attracting and keeping employees.

Public stock also provides shareholders increased liquidity for their holdings through the ability to sell shares when an exit strategy is desired.

DISADVANTAGES OF GOING PUBLIC

Disadvantages of going public are primarily high costs and diminished control over the company. Costs of going public include printing, attorneys, accountants, filing fees, and underwriter commissions. This is expensive, even if a business uses one of the more affordable options such as Reg A+ or Reg D (discussed later in this chapter).

In addition, going public increases a business's ongoing administrative costs. Going public has always meant more regulations to follow and more paperwork to process. Public corporations undergo extensive auditing and must gather and distribute or otherwise make available periodic financial and nonfinancial information to their shareholders and to the general public. They must also comply with a host of regulations adopted in the aftermath of the Great Depression and the Great Recession. These additional administrative functions add to the overall cost of doing business and require the business to be conducted in a "fishbowl." In other words, public companies are subject to intense public scrutiny in addition to that of investors and state and federal regulators.

The Sarbanes-Oxley Act was enacted in July 2002 after major accounting frauds were revealed at some of the country's largest corporations. This act, which mandated a number of reforms to combat corporate and accounting fraud, regulates, among other things, how companies report financial results and disclose executive compensation. The law requires companies and their auditors to prepare detailed documentation of procedures for assuring the accuracy of their financial statements—resulting in significantly increased costs for most public companies. Some smaller companies are, however, eligible for reduced reporting requirements.

In Plain English

While shareholders supply much-needed capital to a growing business, they also usurp a degree of control over the company's operations. Suddenly, management is beholden to a large number of investors, whose interest in short-term profits might conflict with what's best for the long-term health of the business.

Shareholders and the general public (including competitors) must also be apprised of previously private information, including details about management, organization, executives, products, sales, and profit figures. Public disclosure of this information can put a business at a competitive disadvantage. Furthermore, minority shareholders have certain dissenter and minority rights that give them a voice disproportionate to the size of their ownership interests.

FEDERAL AND STATE SECURITIES LAWS

The Securities and Exchange Commission (SEC), created in 1934, is responsible for administering federal securities laws. Its purpose is to assure equal access to and full disclosure of all material facts about a business. However, the SEC recognizes that the burden of disclosure is often excessive and nonessential as applied to smaller businesses, so special procedures and exemptions have been established for smaller businesses to simplify and expedite the registration process.

A "Reg A+ offering" or "mini IPO" is a streamlined process allowing companies to raise up to $75 million in a twelve-month period. According to one law firm that handles Reg A+ offerings, a Reg A+ offering generally costs between $275,000 and $450,000, excluding commissions, in early 2021. If the amount of capital is $10 million or less, you may be eligible for the Small Corporate Offering Registration (SCOR) through Rule 504 of Regulation D. This more affordable option requires you to file in each state in which you want to sell securities, so it's best for localized offerings.

In most cases, a securities issuer must also comply with state provisions known as "blue sky" laws. These laws are sometimes more stringent than the federal statutes, which may offset the benefits of simplified procedures and exemptions under federal law. Compliance with these state and federal laws—even those applicable to the simplified procedures—is highly technical. Only experienced securities attorneys are in a position to counsel you about the requirements of a particular transaction.

Violations of securities laws can result in civil and, in some cases, criminal, liability. Sanctions include rescission of the entire offering, money damages, injunction against or voiding of business transactions, and even criminal prosecution. Further, all securities, whether registered or exempt, are subject to strict anti-fraud provisions. Liability of the issuer is unlimited and extends to significant shareholders, as well as to other related persons or entities. Because of this, you'll need to have your attorney determine whether an appropriate exemption from securities compliance is available in your situation or whether you must undertake the time-consuming and expensive process of registering the securities you plan to issue.

Initial Public Offering

Deciding when and how to go public is time-consuming and complicated. A company must first determine whether it's in an appropriate position to make a public offering and then choose the optimal timing. Factors to consider include the availability of other means of financing, the degree of financial need, and the market conditions for the business's specific product or services being offered. Since an initial offering of securities—whether an IPO, a mini IPO or a SCOR offering—is extraordinarily complex, you'll need to assemble a professional team to assist with the myriad legal and financial considerations that are inherent in the process. This support team typically includes experienced securities and corporate legal counsel, independent accountants, investment bankers, underwriters, and selling agents.

Attorney's Role

The complex nature of securities law makes an experienced securities attorney an indispensable part of any successful public offering. The attorney must ensure compliance with all relevant laws and regulations. The attorney must also make the company aware of possible exemptions, advise on necessary disclosures, and assist in preparing those documents—such as a prospectus or offering memorandum and a registration statement. Furthermore, an experienced securities attorney can review existing contracts and recommend changes, file documents for SEC review, and suggest internal structural changes to ease the company's transition from private to public.

Accountant's Role

A significant part of any public offering is the accounting required by the SEC. External accountants must provide audits of the company to ensure that all financial data is accurate and current, and, when appropriate, prepare earnings projections or forecasts. The accountant works closely with the attorney during the registration process.

Banker's Role

Many companies need interim or bridge financing before the offering is completed, and a banker might assist with this interim financing. Many companies are funded by a combination of financing vehicles, such as conventional loans, lines of credit secured by inventory or accounts receivable or both, and traditional equity financing (stock). The banker should assist the company in determining its optimum funding mix and in obtaining loans when appropriate.

Underwriters' and Selling Agents' Roles

Rarely is a company in a position to sell its own securities, so an underwriter is retained to place the investment. Underwriters usually have a network of sales agents who assist them in selling the company's securities. Generally, there are three kinds of underwriting.

- **Firm underwriting**—the underwriter purchases the entire offering at a discount and resells it to investors. This is customarily used for very large, established companies with an existing public market.
- **Standby underwriting**—the underwriter commits to sell a certain amount of the offering and agrees to purchase up to that portion if it's not sold to investors. Again, this form of underwriting is customarily confined to large established companies with an existing public market in their securities.
- **Best efforts underwriting**—the underwriter agrees to use its best efforts to sell the offering. There's no assurance that any securities will actually be sold. Nor is the underwriter obligated to purchase unsold securities. This is the most common type of underwriting for IPOs, smaller companies, and private placements.

CROWDFUNDING

Crowdfunding refers to a financing method in which money is raised through soliciting relatively small individual investments or contributions from a large number of people. You can avoid securities compliance by using a crowdfunding platform like Kickstarter, Indiegogo, and Patreon, but this method doesn't allow you to offer equity in exchange for the funding. Instead, you have to convince people to donate just because they want to help, or for a reward such as a some of the vegan bacon being developed or early access to your baking podcast.

If you want to offer equity in exchange for the investment (securities-based crowdfunding), you must comply with the federal securities laws, though Regulation Crowdfunding (Reg CF) allows companies to offer and sell up to $5 million of their securities in a twelve-month period without having to register the offering with the SEC.

Reg CF allows eligible companies to offer and sell securities through crowdfunding, provided that all transactions under Reg CF take place online through an SEC-registered intermediary (either a broker-dealer or a funding portal) and appropriate disclosures are made. Further, the amount individual investors can invest across all crowdfunding offerings in a twelve-month period is limited, and securities purchased in a crowdfunding transaction generally can't be resold for one year.

GOING PRIVATE

While many companies go public in order to satisfy business and other needs, numerous previously publicly traded companies have reverted to being private again. The process of a public company going private (sometimes referred to as "going dark" because of the lack of provision of public financial and non-financial information) is complex but typically involves a situation where an individual company or group offers to purchase the stock or ownership interest from public holders for a price that exceeds the then-trading price of that security. The process of taking a business private is as technical and demanding as the process of taking it public. Compliance with the laws surrounding so-called tender offers and the rules imposed by the SEC also requires the skills of experienced securities lawyers, accountants, and other professionals.

In Plain English

Determining whether your business must comply with some or all of the federal and state securities laws is essential. Work with an experienced securities attorney, accountant, and business advisor in order to make this determination and avoid the undesirable consequences that can result from violating the securities laws.

CHAPTER 6

Contracts

Contracts are an essential part of virtually every business. Clearly, we can't cover the entire field of contract law here, but by becoming aware of some of the ramifications of contract law, you'll see where you need to be cautious.

CONTRACT BASICS

A contract is a legally binding promise or set of promises. The law requires the parties to a contract to perform the promises they've made to each other. In the event of nonperformance—usually called a breach—the law provides remedies to the injured party. For purposes of this discussion, we'll assume that the contract is between two people, though contracts can involve any number of parties and frequently involve business organizations. When business organizations are involved, there are additional considerations that complicate the analysis. These include whether the person acting on behalf of the business has appropriate authority and whether that individual's act is within the scope of the business. Discuss these issues with your business attorney.

The three basic elements of every contract are the offer, the acceptance, and the consideration. To illustrate these elements, suppose a restaurant patron orders a salad (the offer). The server brings the salad (the acceptance). The price was stated on the menu (the consideration). That's the basic framework, but a great many variations can be played on that theme.

TYPES OF CONTRACTS

Contracts can be express or implied, oral or written. While you probably know what "oral" and "written" contracts are, you might not know the difference between "express" and "implied" contracts.

Express Contracts

An express contract is one in which all the details are spelled out. It can be oral or written, but it's best to put your understanding in writing. For example, you might make a contract with a retail store for you to deliver six dozen cases of your brewery's seasonal pumpkin beer on September 15, at a price of twelve dollars per case, to be paid within thirty days of receipt. This scenario is fairly straightforward. If either party fails to live up to any material part of the contract, a breach has occurred. The other party may withhold performance of its obligation until receiving assurance that the breaching party will perform. In the event that assurance isn't provided, the aggrieved party may have a cause of action and sue for breach of contract.

If you don't deliver the pumpkin beer until October 1, and the store had advertised the availability of your pumpkin beer during the last week of September, time was an important consideration, and the store wouldn't be required to accept the late shipment. If time isn't a material consideration, then, even with the delay, this probably would be considered substantial performance and the store would have to accept the delivery.

Implied Contracts

Implied contracts usually aren't reduced to writing. An example is where you call a supplier to order one hundred pounds of flour without specifically saying that you'll pay for the flour. Your promise to pay is implied in the order and is enforceable when the flour is delivered.

With implied contracts, however, things often become a lot stickier. Suppose a law firm asks your restaurant to cater a business lunch to try out your services. You deliver a first-class meal, and you overhear the firm's managing attorney commenting how great it is. Is there an implied contract to pay for the meal in this arrangement? That depends on whether you normally give away large free samples of food.

UNDERSTANDING CONTRACT PRINCIPLES

To better understand the principles of offer, acceptance, and consideration, look at these hypothetical situations involving restaurant owner Pat Smith.

- At a reception hosted at the restaurant, Jones expresses an interest in having an event catered by the restaurant. "One of these days, I'll have you cater one of my parties," Jones tells Smith. Is this a contract? If so, what are the terms of the offer? The type of food? The number of people to serve? The price? No, this isn't really an offer that Smith can accept. It's nothing more than a vague expression of intent.
- Brown offers to pay $400 if Smith caters a lasagna and salad lunch the following Thursday for twelve people. The usual charge for this lunch is $450, but Smith agrees to accept the lower price. Is this an enforceable contract? Yes! Brown has offered in unambiguous terms to pay a specific amount for specific services, and Smith has accepted the offer. A binding contract exists.
- One day Jones shows up at Smith's restaurant and offers $4,000 to reserve the restaurant for a private party on a specific day. Smith accepts and agrees that Jones will pay in advance the following day. An hour later Brown shows up and offers Smith $5,000 to reserve the restaurant for the same day. Can Smith accept the later offer? No—a contract exists with Jones. An offer was made and accepted. The fact that the services haven't yet been delivered or paid for doesn't make the contract any less binding.
- Smith asks Green to design a new logo for the restaurant and offers to pay $2,500 if the logo is satisfactory. Green completes the work, but Smith claims the work is unsatisfactory and refuses to pay for it. Is Smith obligated to pay for the logo? No. Here, the offer is conditional upon Smith's satisfaction with the completed work. Green can accept the offer only by producing something that meets Smith's subjective standards—a risky proposition for Green. There's no enforceable contract for payment until Smith indicates that the completed work is satisfactory.

- In the example above, suppose Smith first says the work is satisfactory, but when Green delivers the invoice, Smith expresses second thoughts about the suitability of the logo. That's too late—the contract became binding when Smith said the work is satisfactory, so refusing to accept the logo is a breach of the contract.

PROVING AN AGREEMENT

Contracts are enforceable only if they can be proven, which means oral contracts aren't worth the paper they're written on. The best practice, of course, is to get the contract in writing. This serves not only as proof of the terms agreed to, but also helps the parties clarify the terms of their agreement. Some people prefer to do business on the basis of a handshake, believing the best business relations are those based upon mutual trust. Although there may be some validity to this, business owners should put all agreements in writing. Far too many trusting people have suffered adverse consequences because they relied on the sanctity of oral contracts.

In even the best of business relationships, one or both parties might forget the terms of an oral agreement, or the parties might have very different ideas about the precise terms of the agreement. When the agreement is put into writing, however, there's much less doubt as to the terms of the arrangement. A written contract functions as a safeguard against subsequent misunderstandings or forgetful minds. Proof of oral contracts typically centers around the conflicting testimony of the parties involved. If you can't show that it's more likely than not that your version of the contract is the correct one, then the oral contract might be considered nonexistent. The same result might occur if the parties can't remember the precise terms of the agreement.

Of course, in your food and beverage business, some contracts are nearly always oral, like when a customer makes a reservation (though this is becoming less frequent now that many restaurants and brewpubs accept reservations made online). You might not have thought of a reservation as a contract, but once your restaurant accepts a customer's request for a reservation, legally your restaurant and the customer have a contract. If your restaurant only accepts reservations guaranteed with a credit card, then the contract exists once the customer provides that number. Although you're not likely to require written contracts for reservations, you should have written policies regarding reservations, cancellations, no-shows, and the like and ensure that your staff follows them.

WHEN WRITTEN CONTRACTS ARE NECESSARY

Even if an oral contract is proven to exist, it might not be enforceable. Certain types of contracts must be in writing to be legally enforceable, including:

- any contract that, by its terms, can't be completed in less than one year, and
- any contract that involves the sale of goods for over $500.

An early law designed to prevent fraud and perjury, known as the Statute of Frauds, provides that any contract which, by its terms, can't be fully performed within one year, must be in writing. This rule is narrowly interpreted, so if there's any possibility, no matter how remote, that the contract could be fully performed within one year, the contract doesn't have to be in writing.

For instance, if you agree to cater an office's holiday party each year for a period of five years, the contract has to be in writing. By the terms of the agreement, there's no way the contract could be performed within one year. If, on the other hand, the contract calls for you to cater five events within a period of five years, the Statute of Frauds wouldn't require the contract to be in writing because the five events could occur within the first year. The fact that you don't complete performance of the contract within one year is immaterial. So long as completing performance within one year is within the realm of possibility, the contract can be oral.

The Statute of Frauds further provides that any contract for the sale of goods valued at $500 or more isn't enforceable unless it's in writing and signed by the party against whom enforcement is being sought. The fact that a contract for a price in excess of $500 isn't in writing doesn't void the agreement or render it illegal. The parties are free to perform the oral arrangement, but if one party refuses to perform, the other will be unable to legally enforce the agreement.

The law defines goods as all things that are movable at the time the contract is made, except for the money used as payment. The question is whether a particular contract involves the sale of goods for a price of $500 or more. The answer isn't as clear as you might think. For example, if a supplier agrees to provide your restaurant with all its produce needs for the coming year, how is the price to be determined for purposes of the Statute of Frauds? If the wholesaler delivers produce from several sources and the total purchase price exceeds $500, does the agreement need to be in writing? The safest course is to put all agreements into writing. Most states list additional circumstances requiring contracts to be in writing, so you should contact your attorney before entering into any important oral contract.

ESSENTIALS TO PUT IN WRITING

A contract should be written in simple language that both parties can understand and spell out the terms of the agreement, including, at a minimum:

- the date of the agreement;
- identification of the parties (the buyer and seller in the case of sale of goods or services);
- a description of the goods or services sold;
- the price or other consideration; and
- the signatures of the parties involved.

To supplement these basics, an agreement should spell out whatever other terms might be applicable, such as pricing arrangements, payment schedules, insurance coverage, and when the products/services are to be delivered. Many transactions are important enough that additional clauses covering certain contingencies should be added as well. A written document that leaves out essential terms of the contract presents many of the same problems of proof and ambiguity as an oral contract.

The COVID-19 pandemic has highlighted the importance of "force majeure" clauses in contracts. A force majeure clause excuses one or more of the parties from performing their contractual obligations when specified circumstances beyond their control arise that make their performance commercially impracticable (extremely burdensome), illegal, or impossible. In the past, few of these clauses have specified "pandemics" as an excuse for performance, and it is now clear that references to these, as well as to "epidemics" and "outbreaks," should be included in every force majeure clause.

In Plain English

The terms of a contract should be well thought-out, clearly drafted, conspicuous (e.g., not in tiny print no one can read), and in plain English (or other language used for the contract), so everyone can understand them.

NO-COST WRITTEN AGREEMENTS

But, you might argue, small-business owners often don't have the time, energy, skill, or patience to draft contracts. After all, you're in business to make a product or sell a service, not to draft written contracts steeped in legal jargon. The supplier you're buying from might be willing to draft a contract. Be wary of signing an agreement provided by the other party, especially if it's a form, because it will almost invariably be one-sided, with all terms in favor of whoever drafted it (or paid to have it drafted). As an alternative, you might hire an attorney to draft contracts, but this is usually cost-effective only for large transactions and forms that you can use over and over again. With respect to smaller onetime transactions, the legal fees might be much larger than the benefits derived from having a written contract.

The Uniform Commercial Code ("UCC") provides businesses with a third and, perhaps the best, alternative. The UCC is a body of commercial law adopted in every US state except Louisiana, which hasn't adopted all parts of the UCC, though it has legislation that's comparable to the UCC. While the UCC applies only to the sale of goods, in situations where it applies, businesses don't need to draft contracts or rely on anyone else to do so.

Confirming Memorandum

The UCC provides that an oral contract is enforceable when both parties are merchants and one party sends the other a written confirmation of an oral contract within a reasonable time after that contract was made, so long as the recipient doesn't object to the confirming memorandum within ten days of its receipt. Merchants are those who normally deal in goods of the kind sold or who, because of occupation, represent that they have knowledge or skill peculiar to the services or goods involved in the transaction. Most businesspeople are considered merchants.

The sole effect of the confirming memorandum is that neither party can use the Statute of Frauds as a defense, assuming the recipient fails to object within ten days after receipt. The party sending the confirming memo must still prove that an oral contract was made before or at the same time as the written confirmation. Once such proof is offered, neither party can raise the Statute of Frauds to avoid enforcement of the agreement.

The advantage of the confirming memo over a written contract is that the confirming memo can be used without the active participation of the other contracting party. It would suffice to simply say: "This memo is to confirm our oral agreement," but since you'd still have to prove the terms of that agreement, it would be useful to provide a bit more detail in the confirming memorandum, such as the subject of the contract, the date it was made, and the price or other consideration to be paid. You might draft something like this:

> This memo confirms our oral agreement made on December 12, 2021, pursuant to which Rainbow Valley Hops agreed to deliver to Blue Rhino Brewpub on or before January 12, 2022, fifty pounds of dry Cascade hops for the purchase price of $480.

The advantages of providing some detail in the confirming memorandum are twofold. First, if there's a dispute, you can introduce the memo as proof of the terms of the oral agreement. Second, the memo's recipient won't be allowed to offer evidence of any terms of the oral contract that contradict the terms contained in the memo. The recipient—or, for that matter, the party sending the memo—can introduce proof only regarding the terms of the oral contract that are consistent with the memo's terms. In the above example, you can't argue that the contract called for delivery of seventy pounds of hops, because the quantity (fifty pounds) is in the memo, and Rainbow Valley didn't object. On the other hand, either you or the supplier can testify that the oral contract required Rainbow Valley to deliver the hops using FedEx Ground, since this testimony isn't inconsistent with the memo's terms.

In Plain English

If drafting a complete written contract proves too burdensome or too costly, submit a memorandum in confirmation of the oral contract. This at least surpasses the initial barrier raised by the Statute of Frauds, and by recounting the terms in the memo, you're in a much better position to prove the oral contract later.

Additional Terms

One party to a contract can prevent the other from adding or inventing terms that aren't spelled out in the confirming memorandum by ending the memorandum with a clause requiring all other provisions to be contained in a written and signed document. Such a clause might read as follows.

> This is the entire agreement between the parties and no modification, alteration, or additional terms will be enforceable unless in writing and signed by both parties.

If you use a clause like this, make sure there aren't any terms you agreed to that aren't included in the written document, because a court will generally be confined to the four corners of the document when trying to determine what the parties agreed to. This means that nothing more than what's on the paper containing the agreement will be allowed as evidence. If this language were included in the hop-purchase memo above, neither party could claim the oral contract required shipping by FedEx Ground.

An exception to this rule is that a court may allow oral evidence for the purpose of interpreting ambiguities or explaining the meaning of certain technical terms. The court may also permit the other parties to introduce evidence of past practices in connection with the contract in question, in connection with other agreements between the parties, or even in connection with contracts between other parties.

CONTRACTING ONLINE

The Electronic Signatures in Global and National Commerce Act (ESIGN), passed in 2000, made most e-contracts and e-signatures just as enforceable as their paper counterparts. In addition, all states have laws establishing the validity of electronic signatures and contracts. An e-contract is created and signed electronically. Online purchases are also a form of e-contract. Without signing anything, the buyer agrees to pay the seller a specified amount in exchange for the seller's promise to deliver certain products or services to the buyer.

When e-signing a contract, you might type your name or initials into the signature area, paste in a scanned version of your pen-and-ink signature, or click an "I accept" button. Often, people enclose typed e-signatures with slashes (e.g., /Leonard D. DuBoff/ or /cak/. "Digital signatures" are a more secure form of e-signatures that use digital identification to authenticate the signer. The signature is then electronically bound to the document using encryption.

E-Signature and E-Contract Requirements

Certain measures are typically required to make e-contracts and e-signatures valid and enforceable. These usually include obtaining consent from signers, clearly informing signers that they're agreeing to be bound to the terms of a document when they sign, and letting signers know they can withdraw their consent to e-signatures or e-contracts. In addition, the party creating the contract must keep electronic or paper copies of the signed documents and either provide copies to the other party or let the party know how to get them. No special technology has to be used for online contracting. Electronically signed documents can be encrypted if the parties agree. There are a number of companies, including DocuSign and Adobe, that can assist you with online contracts.

CONSUMER PROTECTION LAWS

The federal government and all the states have enacted legislation designed to give consumers the opportunity to change their minds and cancel unwanted sales. In effect, consumers are given a period of time during which to determine whether they really want to go through with the transaction. If the transaction is canceled within the specified time period, the consumer is entitled to a refund of all money paid and allowed to back out of any contract signed without further obligation.

The federal "cooling off" law generally applies to any sale, loan, or rental of consumer goods or services at a cost of twenty-five dollars or more, but only when the seller personally solicits the sale. In addition, the buyer's agreement, or offer to purchase, must have been made at a place other than the seller's normal place of business—for example, a sale made at the buyer's home or a trade show. However, there are exceptions, including sales at public car auctions and craft fairs.

The seller's principal obligation under these regulations is to notify potential consumers that this cooling-off period exists and that they have the right to cancel the sale if desired. The form and content of this disclosure requirement is spelled out in the applicable regulations. Essentially, the notice-of-cancellation form must explain the buyer's rights and obligations in the event the buyer chooses to cancel the sale. If you engage in consumer sales other than from a permanently established business location, confer with an attorney who can advise you of the legal requirements in your state for your specific situation.

ONLINE AND MAIL-ORDER SALES

If you solicit sales online or through the mail, you must reasonably expect to be able to ship any ordered merchandise to the buyer within the time stated or implied by the solicitation. If no time period is given, you must reasonably expect to ship the merchandise within thirty days after receiving a properly completed order. If you're unable to ship the merchandise within the specified time limit, you must offer the buyer the option of either consenting to a delay in shipping or of canceling the order and receiving a prompt refund. You must also inform the buyer of any anticipated delays in shipping and explain why you can't meet the shipping deadline.

CONSIGNMENT

Food and beverage businesses typically buy and sell on an outright purchase basis, but there are situations where you might need to know the legal requirements for consignment sales. Perhaps your restaurant decorates its walls with artwork consigned by local artists, your tasting room has a gift shop with souvenirs consigned by craftspeople, or maybe you're just starting a baked goods business and are trying to get your foot in the door at a local coffee cart by offering your breakfast pastries on a consignment basis.

The purchaser of an item owns it outright and has complete control over the price and terms of resale, but it also has to advance the purchase price. In consignment, on the other hand, the "consignee" doesn't have to pay for the item up front, but it doesn't own the item. If the item is sold, the consignee will owe a commission (usually a percentage of the sales price) to the "consignor." The consignee usually isn't obligated to sell the goods and can return them at any time.

While there are many advantages to consignment, there are a number of potential problems that should be addressed in a written contract, including insurance and how the consignee's creditors will be made aware that the items are held on consignment, not owned by the consignee. Since a consignee's creditors might be misled into believing the consignee owns these goods, the UCC says that where a consignor delivers an item to a business dealing in goods of the kind consigned, the consignor doesn't have priority over the claims of creditors or a trustee in bankruptcy unless the consignor complies with specific requirements.

In addition, many states have special consignment laws for artwork. Don't just assume these laws don't apply to your business because your primary source of revenue is selling food and beverages. Most of these laws define "art dealer" as anyone engaged in the business of selling artwork other than a person exclusively engaged in the business of selling goods at public auction, so a coffee shop selling the art decorating its walls is considered to be an art dealer. Check with your attorney for the proper procedures in your state if you're involved in consignment sales, whether as the consignor or the consignee.

CHAPTER 7

Collections

Ways to deal with collection problems range from preventive action to initiating a lawsuit. If you're fortunate enough to deal with people who always pay their bills on time, the remainder of this chapter may be of no interest at all. If, however, you've experienced delays in payment, bad checks, stolen credit card numbers, or the like, consider the suggestions that follow.

POINT-OF-SALE PAYMENTS

Makers of food and beverage products who deal directly with the public at shows, fairs, or their own shops usually expect to be paid when they make the sale, before the item is taken away by the customer. In the case of restaurants, tap houses, wine-tasting rooms, and the like, payment might not be expected before the customer receives the purchased items, but it's still expected before the customer leaves the premises. Though more and more people are using digital wallets to pay, point-of-sale payments are most frequently made with cash, check, credit card, or debit card, so you or your staff will need to determine whether currency is authentic and whether cards and checks are likely to be honored by the bank.

Currency

Identifying good counterfeit currency is highly technical, but occasionally counterfeiters make glaring errors, so you and your employees should take a careful look at all bills. The best way to avoid being stuck with a counterfeit bill is to familiarize yourself with real currency (its look and feel, including paper quality, security threads, and watermarks) and to use one of the special pens that can detect most counterfeit US currency. Also, it's a good idea to refuse to accept any bill larger than a fifty-dollar bill. Keep an eye on your local news, as the US Secret Service and local police departments issue alerts when they're aware of counterfeit currency in an area.

Debit and Credit Cards

With regard to debit and credit cards, if you're still using a method requiring paper signatures, the first thing to do is to compare the signature on the back of the card with the signature on the credit card slip. If you haven't already, consider upgrading to chip readers. Cards with magnetic stripes are relatively easy to "clone," but the EMV computer chip prevents cloning and helps prevent theft of the card using a skimmer.

EMV-compliant merchants aren't required to collect signatures for credit and debit card purchases. Another motivation for you to switch to EMV equipment is that if a merchant has only a magstripe reader and a customer presents a stolen or fraudulent card with both a magstripe and a chip, you'll be responsible for the loss on the purchase. If you have an EMV card reader, the credit card company is responsible for the loss.

It's also important for you to follow the credit card processing networks' procedures and PCI Security Council standards carefully. It may seem time-consuming and troublesome, but if you make a credit-card or debit-card sale without doing so and the card turns out to have been stolen or the buyer has exceeded the card's credit limit, you're likely to be stuck with the loss. It's also an excellent idea to request some form of photo ID to verify that the person you're dealing with is the actual card owner, though you should be aware that identity theft is rampant. Some major processing networks, including Visa and Mastercard, require merchants to accept a card even if the person refuses to show ID, so long as the card is signed.

Be very careful when taking credit card numbers over the telephone and online. Always get the Card Verification Value (CVV number) and verify that there's an AVS match. AVS is an address verification system that matches your customer information with the information on file with the card issuer. The same care is necessary when accepting payments from digital wallets, whether device-based (for instance, Apple Pay and Samsung Pay) or Internet-based (like Paypal and Google Pay).

Personal Checks

A host of things can prevent a check from being honored or cashed by a bank. To begin with, the person who writes the check might be using a checkbook that belongs to someone else. To reduce the likelihood of this, insist upon seeing at least two pieces of identification, one of which should contain a photograph of the person. A current credit card or a check guarantee card with a photograph and signature facsimile or any other photo ID should serve this purpose. Don't accept as identification Social Security cards, library cards, or any other ID that can be easily obtained or forged.

Watch while the person signs the check (otherwise, the signature might have been previously traced from a valid signature or retained when the check was "washed" to erase the amount payable and the payee) and compare the signature with that of the other identification. While only an expert can identify a good forgery, most people can recognize a clumsy attempt by an amateur. Don't take checks made out to someone else and endorsed to you. Also watch out for counterfeit checks. Is the Magnetic Ink Character Recognition (MICR) line missing? Or printed with shiny or raised ink? Do the colors smear when touched with a damp finger?

Assuming that the individual writing the check is the person whose name is on the check, there are still more potential problems. One of the most common difficulties is the problem of insufficient funds to cover the check or even checks written on closed accounts. If the amount of your sale is substantial, it's prudent to request a certified or bank-guaranteed check. However, requiring the purchaser to have a check certified isn't practical for most retailers.

People you know are less likely to give you a bad check. Even if the buyer is a stranger, the risk of receiving a bad check and not being able to locate the buyer afterward can be reduced if the buyer's address and phone number are copied onto the check from the supporting pieces of identification when they're different from those printed on the face of the check. Don't cash checks or accept checks written for more than the amount owed.

If you accept a lot of checks, consider using an electronic check verification service. Some of these services merely flag accounts and people who have a history of writing bad checks; others verify that the bank account is open, in good standing, and has a positive balance. Some even guarantee payment if they fail to alert you to a bad check. Some check-processing services allow you to use a check reader or image to convert the check to an e-check. The service verifies the check and transfers the funds from the customer's account to yours. Services using Automated Clearing House (ACH) processing can be used with traditional paper checks or totally electronic checks (as in direct deposits and online bill-pay).

Despite all these precautions, some bad checks do slip through. In most states, it's a crime to pay for something with a check that the signer knows will be dishonored, and you can sue a buyer to recover the amount of the check. If you win, most states allow you to recover your reasonable costs of litigation, including the attorney's fees incurred.

In Plain English

Some bad checks are simply the result of a miscalculation of account balance or of the buyer having received a bad check. It is always a good idea to make a phone call before filing a lawsuit.

INVOICING

The other method of payment is to submit an invoice to a wholesale buyer. Invoices are commonly paid within a specified time, usually thirty days after they have been tendered. This system virtually guarantees that you won't receive payment until the invoice is due. Indeed, unless some inducement for early payment is offered, you may wait interminably to be paid.

Ways of Encouraging Payment

You can encourage debtors to pay their obligations promptly by offering benefits for timely payment, imposing penalties for late payment, or both.

1. Cash Discounts

By offering a cash discount, you can encourage early payment in a simple way. The offer of a 5 percent cash discount for early (or even on-time) payment is all the encouragement some purchasers need.

2. Charging Interest on Overdue Payments

Another option, which can be combined with the incentive of cash discounts, is to charge interest on payments received after the invoice due date, but this method involves two possible traps. First, many states have usury laws limiting the percentage of interest you can charge. If you exceed the legal interest ceiling, you may find you've forfeited all interest or even the entire debt. You might also have to pay a usury penalty. Check with your attorney to make sure the rate you charge complies with any applicable laws.

The second possible problem is compliance with the federal Truth-in-Lending Act (TILA) and the various equivalent state laws. TILA requires certain terms be included on any contract or billing if (1) you offer credit to consumers, (2) you offer consumer credit on a regular basis, (3) the credit is subject to interest or is payable by written agreement in more than four installments, and (4) the credit is primarily for personal, family, or household purposes. Generally, if you charge interest only for late payments and don't make installment sales, you won't need to worry about TILA, but if compliance is required, use compliance software or preprinted forms containing the required disclosures.

WHEN PAYMENT NEVER COMES

If your efforts to get paid are ineffective, you have several other options.

Do Nothing

The first possibility is to do nothing. If the amount is small enough, you might simply decide not to pursue collection. Needless to say, if this alternative is selected, you should refrain from doing any future business with that customer. Incidentally, there are tax implications for the person whose debt is being written off and, depending on the amount of debt written off, you may be required to issue a form 1099-C to the debtor.

Collection Agencies

A second option is to hire a collection agency to attempt to collect the debt. Collection agencies usually charge a commission of up to 50 percent of the recovered amount, though some charge a fixed fee and others charge a smaller up-front fee and take a lower percentage. Choose your collection agency wisely since it could get you into trouble. If the collection agency uses unlawful debt collection practices, for instance, you might also be liable for damages and penalties.

Lawsuits

A third option is the instigation of a full-scale lawsuit to force payment. Note that in many states, a formal demand for payment must be made before bringing a lawsuit. This option is practical only if the outstanding debt is relatively large, since you'll have to hire an attorney, and the case will likely be expensive, especially if it proceeds all the way to trial.

The court fees charged for filing a case can be rather high, usually several hundred dollars or more. The defendant (the debtor) must be personally served with court papers, which can easily cost a hundred dollars or more per defendant, depending on the difficulty of service. Lastly, if the case is won and the buyer still refuses to pay, further proceedings must be initiated at added cost to execute the judgment (force the debtor to pay). All in all, on a moderate debt, the expense involved in a civil trial can easily amount to more than the debt itself.

Small Claims Court

A simpler and less-expensive solution on small debts is to bring an action in small claims court. While the rules vary from state to state, small claims courts are geared toward making the process as swift, accessible, and inexpensive as possible. Plus, most small claims courts have staff members who help guide people through the process. The major cost savings in a small-claims proceeding results from the fact that attorneys aren't usually permitted to appear in these courts or to prepare documents for filing. Exceptions include attorneys representing themselves or a business entity. Even in states where attorneys aren't specifically barred, the court rules are set up in such a clear, comprehensible way that an attorney usually isn't needed.

Not all actions can be brought in small claims court. As the name implies, only claims for small amounts can be brought. For example, small is defined as $5,000 or less in many states, although as of the date of this writing, maximum claims range from $2,500 to $25,000. In addition, only actions seeking monetary damages are appropriate in small claims court. Other forms of relief, such as an injunction, can't be granted.

The small-claims process is relatively swift and inexpensive. Filing fees are typically under a hundred dollars, and the creditor usually isn't responsible for informing the debtor that a suit has been brought. The clerk of the court customarily mails the notice to the defendant by certified or registered mail. The hearing itself is simple, and the technical rules of evidence and legal procedure aren't followed. The judge simply hears both sides of the case and allows all evidence, including the testimony of any witnesses, that either party has to offer. Jury trials are never permitted in small claims court, although the defendant may be able to have the case moved to a conventional court by demanding a jury trial.

An action in small claims court also has disadvantages. The judgment is often absolutely binding, which means neither party can appeal. Plus, the judgment might be uncollectible. This is because in many states, the usual methods of enforcing a judgment—garnishment of wages or liens against property—are unavailable to the holder of a judgment from small claims court. Some jurisdictions allow a small claims court judgment to be converted into a traditional judgment, but this often requires the help of an attorney to assist with the process, which increases your costs. If, however, all other methods fail, small claims court is by far the least expensive and easiest way to obtain legal redress for a small outstanding debt.

Bankruptcies

When a bankruptcy petition is filed, the debtor is responsible for filing an accurate list of creditors with the court. The court sends a notice of the filing to the listed creditors as well as to all parties who are listed with the court or who make an appearance in the case. Even if the amount at stake in the bankruptcy is small and it seems that it might not be economically practical to pursue the matter, you should file a claim if the court gives notice to do so. Many creditors fail to file claims, often increasing the payment to those who do. There are three general categories of bankruptcies.

In Plain English

Because bankruptcy law is quite technical, you should work with an experienced lawyer if you receive notice that a debtor has filed bankruptcy or if you're considering filing bankruptcy. Experienced lawyers may even be able to avoid a bankruptcy by negotiating a "work out plan," which may result in creditors accepting less than they're owed in order to avoid receiving much less—or even nothing—in bankruptcy.

1. Straight Bankruptcy—Chapter 7

The first, referred to as straight bankruptcy in Chapter 7 of the bankruptcy law, contemplates the prompt conversion of all the bankrupt's nonexempt property to cash and the payment of creditors to the extent possible. This type is available to both individuals and business entities. The bankruptcy law establishes a pecking order of creditors, giving some creditors priority for payment. Such creditors include the US government for taxes and secured parties for the amount of their security interests. Each category of creditor must be paid in full before a lower-priority creditor is paid at all. If there's not enough money to satisfy all creditors in a particular class, each member of that group receives a pro rata share of its claim.

Not all of the bankrupt's assets are available for creditors. Some things can be retained even after bankruptcy—for example, a modest house, a holy book, and clothing. The list of exempt property varies from state to state, though there are federal exemptions, too. In some states, the debtor can choose whether to use the state or federal exemptions. Some exemptions, such as Social Security, aren't part of the bankruptcy laws but may nevertheless apply. Due to these exemptions, very few Chapter 7 cases result in meaningful payments to creditors.

If no one objects to the debtor's discharge or to the discharge of certain types of debt before the deadline set by the court, the court enters an order of discharge preventing creditors from pursuing their claims against the debtor. Some claims can't be discharged in bankruptcy. Some claims remain intact with no action on the part of the creditor (such as certain categories of tax debts and clear support obligations). Other claims (such as fraud and intentional injury) require the filing of a complaint with the bankruptcy court before the discharge deadline.

2. Reorganization—Chapter 11

The second type of bankruptcy proceeding, Chapter 11 (or reorganization), is used primarily by business entities, not individuals. It contemplates a somewhat different process. Instead of dissolving the business, Chapter 11 facilitates an orderly payment to creditors so that the business can survive.

After a Chapter 11 petition is filed and the creditors meet, a reorganization plan is proposed by the debtor, though after a certain period of time, any party can propose a plan. Once a plan is prepared, it's presented to the bankruptcy judge. If the judge determines that the plan meets the requirements of the Bankruptcy Code and the creditors have had an opportunity to vote on the plan, the court may confirm the plan. This is true in some circumstances even when certain creditors vote no, so long as the court determines that the plan is fair, equitable, and doesn't unfairly discriminate.

Creditors customarily receive more under Chapter 11 than they do under straight bankruptcy, although reorganization is feasible only for a healthy business suffering a temporary economic reversal. Creditors who have secured positions, such as those who have filed UCC documents to establish their security interests, can participate in drafting the Chapter 11 plan. Generally, these are creditors who sold on consignment or retain a security interest for the purchase price of some goods. The plan will be "fair and equitable" insofar as the secured creditors are concerned, and they may be forced to agree, if it provides that they do any one of the following:

- retain their liens and receive future cash payments equal to the value of the security;
- retain a lien on the proceeds from the sale of their collateral; or
- receive the equivalent of their interests, like cash up front or substituted collateral.

In a Chapter 11 proceeding, a secured creditor might be forced to accept a less favorable position than the UCC would allow so that all the creditors accept the plan, but someone with a security interest is still far better off than one who is unsecured.

3. Individuals—Chapter 13

Individuals can file Chapter 13 bankruptcies. In this type of arrangement, a three- to five-year plan is worked out so that any amounts the person filing bankruptcy earns over and above the amounts required for ordinary and necessary living expenses are paid to a trustee for ultimate distribution to creditors. To participate in that distribution, a creditor must file a "proof of claim" on a form available from the court.

In Plain English

There will probably always be some uncollectible bills, but with proper care and some preventive attention, you can keep these to a minimum.

CHAPTER 8

Franchises and MLM Companies

Most successful businesses begin with a novel idea that is nurtured and grows into a profitable enterprise. The entrepreneur invests time, money, and energy into developing the concept, perhaps an innovative theme, unusual menu, or new gourmet food product, and might want to expand the business. When you begin considering running your own food and beverage business, you'll need to decide whether you'd prefer to start your own business, buy a preexisting business or an ownership interest in one, purchase a franchise, or participate in a multilevel marketing company.

FRANCHISING

Franchises are a good option for many food and beverage businesses, particularly restaurants. The best source for researching franchises is the Internet. Attending franchise expos, where a number of companies offering franchises present opportunities, is another method of gathering information. There are also books on franchising available at public libraries and bookstores. The Federal Trade Commission (FTC) has adopted specific rules for all companies offering franchise opportunities, and many states have their own franchise regulations as well. For example, a number of states require franchise opportunities to be registered before a franchise opportunity is sold to residents of that state. A typical franchise statute defines a franchise as an agreement by which:

- a franchisee is granted the right to sell goods or services under a marketing system formulated by a franchisor;
- the operation of the franchisee's business pursuant to such a system is substantially associated with the franchisor's trademark, service mark, trade name, logo, advertising, or other commercial symbol designating a franchisor; and
- the franchisee is required to give the franchisor a payment or something else of value (in legal terms, "consideration") for the right to transact business in accordance with the marketing plan. This typically consists of an initial franchise fee and ongoing royalty payments.

Franchise Disclosure Document

All companies that offer franchise opportunities must comply with FTC requirements, including preparing an extensive disclosure statement known as a Franchise Disclosure Document (FDD). By law, a franchisor must furnish prospective franchisees with an FDD at least fourteen calendar days before the prospective franchisee signs a binding agreement with, or makes any payment to, the franchisor or an affiliate in connection with the proposed franchise sale. You'll find a wealth of material in the FDD, including the following background information about the franchisor:

- its parents, predecessors, and affiliates and a number of details about the franchisor and its predecessors and affiliates, including any lawsuits and bankruptcies they've been involved in;
- the business experience of the management team, including directors, principal officers, and individuals with management responsibility relating to the sale or operation of franchises (whether employed by the franchisor, or an affiliate or parent company), as well as any litigation or bankruptcies they've been involved in;
- the involvement of any celebrities or other public figures in the franchise;
- details of the franchisor's relevant intellectual property (trademarks, copyrights, patents, and proprietary information);

- franchised and corporate outlets over the past three years and a projection of openings in the next year, along with a number of details about all outlets; and
- financial performance representations, the basis for those representations, and the franchisor's financial statements;

You'll also learn about the rights and obligations of franchisees, including

- the contracts you'll have to sign and a brief summary of their requirements;
- an estimated initial investment, including the initial franchise fee and any other payments required to obtain the franchise as well as build-out expenses and reserve capital;
- the continuing payments franchisees are required to make after acquiring a franchise;
- whether the franchisor offers any financing to franchisees, and if so, the terms of that financing;
- any restrictions on the source or quality of goods and services used in the franchise;
- the training and assistance available to franchisees from the franchisor;
- advertising requirements and any mandatory computer and software systems;
- restrictions on the goods and services franchisees are permitted to market;
- any territorial limitations or protections;
- the conditions under which the franchisor can repurchase or refuse renewal of the franchise;
- the conditions under which the franchisee can transfer the franchise to a third party;
- when and how the franchise can be terminated or modified;
- how disputes are to be resolved; and
- the extent to which franchise owners must personally participate in the operation of a franchise.

After reviewing all of the information in the FDD, ask the franchisor any additional questions you have about the opportunity. Some franchisors allow other franchisees to operate in close geographical proximity, or even operate their own locations in close proximity to franchisees. This is known in the trade as cannibalizing—determine whether you have any protection from this practice. Carefully evaluate all the information with a critical eye and determine whether the franchisor's system seems to be workable and worth the franchise fee.

Advantages and Disadvantages

You must decide whether you're willing to acquire a franchise rather than create your own business identity. There are pros and cons to both approaches.

By buying a franchise, you'll obtain the right to follow an established, successful pattern. It also allows you to use the trademarks, recipes, advertising, and training the franchisor provides. Those who purchase franchise opportunities are often more likely to succeed than those who start from scratch, since many of the mistakes that dissipate resources are avoided. The purchaser of a franchise is literally acquiring the goodwill, know-how, and intellectual property of an established business.

One of the major sacrifices to be made when acquiring a franchise opportunity is that of creating your own business identity and perhaps later franchising it to others. By acquiring a franchise, you're purchasing some degree of security in exchange for the potential you might have realized from your own venture.

The purchase of a franchise ranks as a significant investment. Before you make that investment, carefully review all available information, consult a franchise attorney and accountant, and contact other franchisees to learn about their experiences with the franchisor.

MULTILEVEL MARKETING

Another method of doing business is multilevel marketing (MLM). The leading companies in this field have surpassed billion-dollar sales marks and their stocks are traded on the New York Stock Exchange. Amway, LuLaRoe, and Pampered Chef are MLMs that have become household names. MLMs market everything from computers and clothing to food and beverage products like meal kits, wine, spices, sauces, tea, coffee, and chocolate.

Simply stated, multilevel marketing is a form of marketing in which distributors or sales representatives sell products directly to consumers. In most cases, distributors purchase the company product at wholesale and profit from the difference between the wholesale and retail prices. In other cases, a distributor functions as a sales representative who takes orders for company products or services—for instance, gourmet condiments—and receives a commission for whatever is sold.

Distributors are entitled to sponsor other sales representatives ("reps") and receive commissions on the sales of the sponsored reps as well as on the sales of any further reps sponsored in a continuous down line. For a successful distributor, the rewards can be substantial.

Any system that offers dramatic rewards and carries with it a low cost of entry tends to attract some of the best and some of the worst individuals. MLM programs often come under the scrutiny of regulators, who find some of these programs to be unlawful pyramid schemes (sometimes called "endless chain" schemes), but other legitimate programs have survived. In a landmark legal decision in 1979, the Amway Corporation prevailed in such a prosecution. This particular decision opened the door to many other legitimate multilevel marketing companies.

Keep in mind, though, that you might not make money even in a legitimate MLM business. A 2018 AARP study found that only 25 percent of people involved in MLMs made a profit, with 47 percent losing money, and the remainder breaking even.

Protective Regulations

As mentioned above, multilevel marketing is closely scrutinized due to rampant abuses. Regulations related to MLM companies in the United States are a constantly changing patchwork of overlapping laws that vary from state to state, in addition to federal laws enforced by the FTC, the Securities and Exchange Commission (SEC), and the US Postal Service. Generally speaking, these statutes prohibit marketing plans that require sales representatives to invest in the company or purchase the right to recruit others for economic gain. "Pyramid" and "endless chain" statutes typically prohibit payment for the right to recruit others for economic gain when the payment is unrelated to the sale of products or services.

What to Look For

Whether you're a would-be participant or an entrepreneur considering starting your own MLM, it's important to ensure the opportunity is lawful.

1. Investment Requirement. The only investment should be a sales or sample kit, or demonstration materials, sold at company cost.

2. Product/Service. The product or service should be of high quality and have a real demand in the marketplace. If the product is one consumed by distributors themselves, it must be one that distributors would want to buy on its own merits, even if they weren't participating in the MLM.

3. Price. The price of the product or service must be competitive and sold to distributors at wholesale or at a substantial discount from the retail price.

4. Purchase Requirements. A legitimate marketing program has no minimum-purchase or inventory requirements.

5. Commissions. Commissions shouldn't be paid for the mere act of sponsoring other distributors.

6. Buyback Policy. The MLM company should repurchase inventory and sales materials in resalable condition from distributors who no longer want to participate in the program.

7. Retail Sales. The focus of the marketing program should be promoting retail sales to nonparticipants.

8. Distributor Activity. Many of the statutes regarding multilevel distribution companies require that distributors perform a bona fide, supervisory, distributive selling or soliciting function in moving the product to the consumer.

9. Earnings Statements. A legitimate MLM program's earnings' representations should be based on a verifiable track record of average earnings of distributors in a particular geographic area.

To be successful in an MLM program, you must be willing to actively promote sales of the product while continuing to recruit individuals to augment your down line. It's only through both activities that you're likely to earn significant returns.

In Plain English

Before agreeing to become a distributor for an MLM company, you should be sold on the product or service itself, not merely the prospect of getting rich from the activities of others. MLM distributing is hard work! The time devoted to this activity can be considerable and may preclude you from developing other business opportunities.

Abuses

If you're considering working with an MLM company, beware of these red flags:

- products that have no real-world marketplace;
- products that are sold at inflated prices;
- plans that result in inventory loading by distributors (requiring consultants to buy more inventory than they can reasonably use or sell);
- substantial cash investment requirements;
- mandatory purchases of peripheral or accessory products or services;
- plans in which distributors are left with substantial unsold inventory upon cancellation of participation;
- plans in which fees are paid to distributors for headhunting and in which the emphasis is on recruitment rather than the sale of products or services; and
- misrepresentations or inflated representations of earnings.

One example of an alleged pyramid scheme in the food and beverage industry is the Success By Health (SBH) MLM program for beverages (like tea and coffee) that contain "medicinal mushrooms." The FTC filed suit against the company and some of its principals, and, as of the date of this writing, the company is temporarily prohibited from doing business while the case continues. The court that issued the order in early 2020 found "compelling evidence that Defendants are operating a pyramid scheme and that they have otherwise engaged in deceptive practices. . . ."

The court held that SBH's own marketing and training materials make clear that affiliates' potential profits from the sale of retail products are trivial and that the real money comes from recruiting other affiliates. Further, SBH allows non-affiliates to purchase goods through its website at wholesale prices, doesn't track whether affiliates are engaging in retail sales, affirmatively encourages inventory loading, has no compliance policies, and adheres to a strict no-refunds policy.

The Internet is riddled with bogus MLM opportunities, and emails about the incredible earnings potential are ubiquitous. The FTC has attempted to identify these schemes, but the rate at which they emerge appears to outpace regulators' resources. Be especially careful with web-based MLM offerings and email MLM spam since it's often impossible to determine the location of the offeror and to obtain any relief when problems arise.

In Plain English

Many states have laws regulating the promotion, advertisement, and sale of business opportunities, including multilevel marketing programs and franchises. Before advertising your business opportunity or buying into someone else's, consult with an attorney experienced in this field of law.

CHAPTER 9

Patents and Trade Secrets

Ordinarily, before a business can achieve a market edge, something must distinguish it from other items in the same general category. Of course, you'll want to protect the "something" that sets your product apart so that others can't exploit its uniqueness. Several bodies of law help you obtain this protection. This chapter and the following two chapters discuss some of these protections.

PATENTS

Patent laws give an inventor the right to prevent others from exploiting (e.g., manufacturing, using, or selling) a patented invention. Generally speaking, a patent is available for any new and useful process, machine, composition of matter, or any new, useful improvement thereof. Examples in the food and beverage industry include an improved carbonation process for beer, a new order management system for a restaurant, and a new device to measure free and total sulfur dioxide in wine.

An invention can't be patented unless it's new, useful, and not obvious. While the definition of "new" isn't as simple as you might think, briefly, an invention isn't new if the invention was patented or described in a printed publication anywhere in the world or on sale or otherwise available to the public before the application is filed. There is, however, an exception for certain disclosures made less than one year before an application for the patent is filed.

This one-year period is intended to function as a grace period that allows the inventor or the inventor's company to market the invention to see whether it's worthwhile to incur the expense of seeking patent protection. A consequence of failing to file a patent application during this one-year period, however, is that the inventor (or the inventor's business entity) is absolutely barred from obtaining a patent.

You may choose to file a provisional patent application because it will grant you a filing date (patent pending status) before one year elapses from "on sale" and "public disclosure" activities, and it will preserve your right to seek foreign patent protection. Discuss the pros and cons of filing a provisional patent application in your particular situation with your patent attorney.

Unfortunately, patents are quite costly and difficult to obtain. It often takes an inordinate period of time for the patent document to be issued, though the US Patent and Trademark Office (USPTO) does provide an opportunity for the inventor to expedite the process in certain limited situations. Also, the period of protection is relatively short—only twenty years from the date of application. Plus, you'll need to file for a patent in any foreign country where you want patent protection because each country administers its own patent system. One exception to this general rule is the European Patent Regime. Tell your patent attorney or agent if you'd like patent protection in any other country.

In Plain English

A patent attorney is a lawyer who has passed the Patent Bar through the USPTO. A patent agent has passed the USPTO exam but isn't a lawyer and can't give legal advice.

TRADE SECRETS

Another form of protection, known as trade secret law, allows exploitation of a particular innovation and may afford even greater protection than copyright (see Chapter 11) or patent laws. Broadly speaking, for data or a concept used in your business to be protectable as a trade secret:

- it must give you a competitive advantage;
- you must have treated it as a secret and continue to do so; and
- it must not be generally known in your industry or business.

The way you use knowledge and information, the specific portions of information you have grouped together, and the mere assembly of information itself may all be trade secrets, even if everything you consider important for your secrets is publicly available information. For instance, if there are numerous methods for producing a certain natural food coloring and you've selected one of them, the mere fact that you have selected this method for your cupcake frosting may itself be a trade secret. The identity of your hop suppliers might be a trade secret, even though they advertise openly. The fact that you've done business with these people and found them to be reliable may make the list of their names a trade secret.

A trade secret can be lost if its owner fails to identify it or take reasonable steps to protect it. Otherwise, trade secret protection is perpetual. In fact, one of the most famous trade secrets is the recipe for Coca-Cola, which is more than 130 years old. Other famous examples of successful trade secret protection are the herb-and-spice mixture used by KFC in its fried chicken recipe and the process for making Krispy Kreme doughnuts.

How to Protect Your Trade Secrets

In this area, a little thought and cleverness goes a long way toward giving you the protection of the trade secret laws.

1. Physical and Digital Security

Label copies, whether tangible or digital, as "confidential" or "trade secret." Keep tangible copies of confidential information in a locked room, safe, or file cabinet, accessible only to employees who need access to that information to properly perform their jobs. It's prudent to establish a procedure for controlling employee access to these copies. Also restrict access to the area where the trade secret is used and take precautions to prevent visitors from peering into the kitchen or production facility where your secret recipes and techniques are used. Take extra care with laptops, tablets, smartphones, and other portable devices, since, if they're lost or stolen, a tremendous amount of data is at risk of disclosure.

Password-protect company networks and all files that include trade secrets. Folders containing trade secret information should be accessible only to those with appropriate login credentials. Consider encrypting the information as well for an extra level of security. Make sure you scrub the drives of any electronic devices (including computers, tablets, scanners, photocopiers, and smartphones) before disposing of them, and teach employees how to avoid phishing scams.

Conduct exit interviews with employees, reminding them of their continuing legal obligations with respect to your company's trade secrets and other confidential information. Also, make sure you get back all of your business's property, including keys and electronic devices. Immediately inactivate their access to your security system, computers, networks, and software.

2. Fragmenting Information

If possible, fragment the information you consider to be a trade secret so that no one person has possession of the entire secret. This is the procedure adopted by KFC—one company creates a blend with its part of the recipe, and a second company adds spices to complete the recipe. In a small restaurant, brewery, or the like, this may be impractical.

3. Confidentiality Agreements

Have all your employees sign a nondisclosure agreement ("NDA") when hired. An attorney who deals with intellectual property can prepare form agreements for use within your business. If you ever need to reveal a secret to an outsider, like an IT consultant or someone who wants a license to make and sell your restaurant's salad dressing, a different form of confidentiality agreement is in order. Again, your intellectual property lawyer can prepare such an agreement for you.

4. Vague Labeling

Another method of protecting your trade secret is to engage in some vague labeling. For instance, if your trade secret consists of a unique mixture of ingredients for a meat glaze, then instead of having the components of the glaze bear their true names, you can label them "Ingredient A," "Ingredient B," "Ingredient C," etc. Then, if a stranger happens into your kitchen, they won't know enough to re-create the recipe.

Employee Trade Secrets

In the food and beverage industry, many chefs, bakers, brewers, vintners, roasters, and the like have their own trade secrets. Whether these trade secrets become the property of your business or remain those of the employee can be negotiated just like salary and benefits. The agreement regarding ownership should be in writing and signed by both parties.

In Plain English

Take care not to inadvertently reveal trade secrets. It's easy to slip up when, for example, you share a recipe on Instagram, talk to a reporter about the grand opening of your new brewpub, chat with friends about your new process for crushing grapes, or write for an industry trade journal.

Misappropriation of Trade Secrets

State and federal laws provide remedies for those whose trade secrets are misappropriated. The federal Defend Trade Secrets Act of 2016 (DTSA) allows an injured business to file suit in federal court, and the Economic Espionage Act of 1996 criminalizes some trade secret misappropriation. If someone misappropriates your trade secrets, you might be eligible for damages, which can be calculated a number of ways, depending on the specific law you sue under. You might be awarded a judgment that covers the amount of money you lost, the "unjust enrichment" received through misappropriation of your trade secrets, exemplary damages of twice the amount of actual damages, or attorney fees, or a combination of these. In addition, the court might issue an injunction prohibiting certain activities.

To reduce the chances of being sued for stealing someone else's trade secrets, question employees who come to work for you from a competitor. If there's any possibility of a new employee using the competitor's trade secret information, the new employee should obtain the former employer's written permission to use the information while working for you. Also have employees promise in writing that they won't use or disclose any trade secret information learned from a former employer or other third party.

PATENT OR PADLOCK DILEMMA

The determination of whether patent or trade secret protection is most appropriate is sometimes referred to as the "patent or padlock dilemma." The same item can't have both kinds of protection. Because a patent application must contain a full description of precisely what was invented, it's impossible to get both a patent and have trade secret protection. If you choose trade secret protection, you can't just change your mind and obtain a patent, because you have to file for a patent within the first year of using the invention for commercial purposes. For help making the best decision for your business, consult an attorney or patent agent who specializes in intellectual property.

CHAPTER 10

Trademarks

Branding has become part of the lexicon of business terms. One of the most important aspects of branding is establishing a means of identifying a product or service by use of a name, symbol, logo, device, or combination of these items, commonly known as a trademark or service mark. A trademark is used to define marks that are affixed to goods. Service marks are used to define marks that are used in connection with services, though people often use the term "trademarks" or "marks" to refer to both trademarks and service marks (and we do so in this book).

Although modern trademark law has broadened the protection available for trademark owners, its historical antecedents date back to medieval England when craft guilds often required members to place their individual marks on the products they produced. It's not surprising that unscrupulous merchants quickly realized that there was easy money to be made by using the marks of quality manufacturers on their own shoddy goods.

In response to this problem of consumer fraud, the first trademark laws developed. Initially, they focused on those who passed off their products as someone else's. In contrast, modern American law focuses upon whether one mark is sufficiently similar to another to cause confusion in the minds of the buying public. The emphasis has shifted from the subjective intent of dishonest manufacturers and merchants passing off their goods as those of another to the more objective determination of consumer confusion. In other words, you can be guilty of trademark infringement even if you didn't intend to mislead anyone.

Despite this shift, the essential purpose of trademarks and trademark laws has changed little since the days of the craft guilds. Trademarks still function primarily as a means of identifying the source of a particular product. Trademark laws are also designed to enable the trademark proprietor to develop goodwill for the product as well as to prevent another party from exploiting that goodwill—regardless of whether that exploitation is intentional or innocent.

DEFINITION

A simplification of the federal definition of a trademark is—

> any word, name, symbol, device, or any combination thereof, used by a person (or which a person has a bona fide intention to use) in commerce to identify and distinguish their goods or services from those manufactured or sold by others and to indicate the source of those goods or services, even if that source is unknown.

The term "use in commerce" means using the mark in the ordinary course of trade—not merely to reserve a right in the mark. You can reserve a mark before using it, but the mark won't be registered until it's been used in commerce.

The key concept of trademark law is that the mark must be distinguishable from other marks or "distinctive." The most distinctive trademarks are those that are either "fanciful" (made-up words like Pepsi, Häagen-Dazs, or Fuddruckers) or arbitrary (a word or phrase used as an identifier for an unrelated product or service, like Blue Lava for coffee beans, Caldera for beer, or Cracker Barrel for a restaurant chain).

Less distinctive are "suggestive" trademarks that imply something about the goods or services but require you to use your imagination to hazard a guess as to the nature of those goods or services. For example, the owners of the Sonic chain of restaurants chose the name because it's associated with speed (their slogan was "Service with the Speed of Sound"). Similarly, Deschutes Brewery's Fresh Squeezed mark, which identifies a citrusy ale, is associated with citrus juice. Although trademarks such as Sonic and Fresh Squeezed aren't purely arbitrary, they're still afforded substantial protection since the marks don't actually describe the goods or services being identified.

PROHIBITED TRADEMARKS

Generic and descriptive names aren't distinctive enough to be granted trademark status. A generic word merely identifies the product for what it is. For instance, "Beer" can't be protected as a trademark for beer—though it might be used as a trademark for tortilla chips or apples. Even less obvious terms may be generic—the US Trademark Trial and Appeal Board (TTAB) found that the mark "Big Six" is generic for wine, because the relevant public understands "big six" primarily to refer to "wines" or a key aspect, type, or ingredient of wines. Similarly, the marks "Hoppy" for India pale ale and "Cheesy Chicken" for a restaurant dish consisting of chicken and cheese are descriptive, because they merely describe the products.

Generic terms never receive trademark protection, though in 2020, the US Supreme Court held that a generic term combined with .com can be protected as a trademark when consumers perceive the mark as a brand name. Based on that decision, which involved the mark booking.com, marks such as restaurants.com or brewpubs.com would likely be protectable. A descriptive trademark can be protected if the mark has acquired a "secondary meaning." Secondary meaning exists when the public no longer connects the words of the trademark with the literal, dictionary meaning, but rather with a unique product or service. For example, "Steak 'N Shake" is the registered trademark of a fast-food restaurant that serves steak and shakes.

Even some distinctive trademarks are prohibited by statute or public policy. For instance, trademarks that are deceptive and misleading, such as the mark Idaho Potatoes to identify potatoes grown somewhere other than Idaho, are denied protection, as are marks identifying a particular living individual (unless you have that person's written consent). A mark is considered to identify a particular living individual if it identifies, to the relevant public, a particular living individual who is well-known or is publicly connected with the business in which the mark is used.

Immoral, disparaging, and scandalous trademarks used to be denied trademark protection, but in cases decided in 2017 and 2019, the US Supreme Court held that these restrictions violate the First Amendment. These types of marks can now be registered so long as they meet the other requirements for protection.

PROTECTING A TRADEMARK

To secure trademark protection, it's not enough merely to adopt a distinctive mark. The trademark must be used in "in commerce," whether you're seeking protection under state or federal law. Registration of a trademark has certain advantages but isn't necessary. Common-law protection, which doesn't require a registration, suffices.

A trademark is "used" when it's placed in any manner on the product, its containers or displays associated with it, or on any of the tags or labels affixed to the product. The trademark doesn't have to be physically affixed to the goods. As long as the mark is associated with the product at the point of sale in such a way that the product is readily identified as coming from a particular manufacturer or source, the mark can be protected. Not every use of a mark is "use" for purposes of trademark law, though. For example, using the trademark on invoices mailed out after accepting a wholesale order might not be sufficient to constitute use, since the trademark isn't associated at the point of sale.

In Plain English

If at all possible, physically affix your trademark to your products so they'll bear the trademark when sold. Proper use of a service mark is accomplished by identifying the service by the mark in advertising, signs, brochures, and the like.

Confusingly Similar

As a trademark proprietor, you're protected against someone else using a trademark that is confusingly similar to yours. What does "confusingly similar" mean? Generally, trademarks are confusingly similar if they're similar in sound or appearance, used with similar goods or services, and marketed throughout similar geographic areas.

On the other hand, if the marks identify unrelated goods or services, or if they're used in different geographic areas, there may be no infringement. For instance, a restaurant chain in the Pacific Northwest could probably adopt and use a trademark already used by a restaurant in Maine, so long as the mark of the Pacific Northwest business doesn't adversely affect the value of the trademark used by the Maine company. Also, a Pacific Northwest restaurant chain could probably adopt and use a trademark used by a Northwest chainsaw manufacturer. In these situations, it's unlikely that the use of the mark by the restaurant chain would confuse Maine restaurant customers or chainsaw purchasers.

Remember that goods or services don't have to be identical for confusion to exist. For example, registration has been denied for beer-related trademarks that are similar to preexisting trademarks for vodka and wine. It's not just other alcoholic drinks that are problematic, though. PepsiCo (owner of the Mountain Dew mark for soft drinks) opposed registration of the mark Ole Smoky Mountain Dew Moonshine for distilled spirits, and Ole Smoky Distillery, LLC, agreed to abandon its application.

Federal Registration

Trademark owners have greater protection under federal or state statutes than under the common law. The federal statute governing trademarks is known as the Lanham Act of 1946, though it has been updated a number of times. Under the Lanham Act as amended, a mark must be used in commerce before it can be registered, though you can file an application for a trademark based on a bona fide intention to use that mark in the future. This reserves and protects a mark for a limited time and to a limited extent prior to its being used in commerce. If the mark isn't used within a certain time period, the trademark registration will be denied.

There are two official registers for trademarks: the Principal Register and the Supplemental Register. Marks registered on the Principal Register enjoy all of the benefits of the trademark law, but marks registered on the Supplemental Register do not. The following sections on how to register a trademark apply to the Principal Register (the Supplemental Register is discussed later in this chapter).

1. Applications Based on Actual Use

Once the owner has established a mark's actual use in commerce, the mark can be registered by filing an application with the US Patent and Trademark Office (USPTO). This entails filling out an application, sending in a drawing of the mark, including specimens of the mark used in commerce, and paying the required fee. As of the date of this writing, the fee ranges from $250 to $50 per international class for electronic applications and $600 for a paper application. For current information, see www.uspto.gov.

If the examining attorney at the USPTO accepts the application, the trademark will be published in the Official Gazette. Anyone who believes they would be injured by registration of the mark has 30 days to file a written notice stating the reasons for opposition. If nobody objects or if the objections are found to be without merit, a certificate of registration is issued.

2. Applications Based on Intent-to-Use

You can reserve a right to a particular mark for future use through an intent-to-use provision by filing an application based on your bona fide intent to use the mark in commerce. In recent years, this bona-fide intent requirement has been much more stringently enforced, and if someone opposes registration (see below), you might have to submit documentary evidence proving that you genuinely intended to use the mark in commerce at the time you filed the application. If your application satisfies all requirements, it receives approval for publication in the Official Gazette, and a thirty-day period for opposition to registration of the mark begins to run. Those applications that go unopposed receive a Notice of Allowance.

Reservation of the mark is limited to a period of six months from the date of allowance, during which time you must begin to use the mark in commerce, or the trademark application will lapse, though you can obtain a six-month extension by applying and paying a fee ($125 per classification of goods or services as of the date of this writing for electronic filings; the fee is $225 for paper filings) so long as you submit the request before expiration. Four additional six-month extensions are possible but require approval by the USPTO upon a showing of good cause why the extension should be granted, plus payment of the fee. You can find the application forms on the USPTO's website at www.uspto.gov. Once you've used the mark in commerce, you'll need to file a verified statement of use and pay a fee (as of the date of this writing, $100 for electronic filings and $200 for paper filings). If everything is in order, the mark is registered for the goods or services that the statement of use indicates.

Filing an application for registration constitutes use of the mark as of the filing date, assuming that the mark is ultimately registered on the Principal Register. This means that if you file your intent-to-use application on September 1, 2021, but you don't use the mark until January 10, 2022, your rights to the mark are based on a "constructive use" date of September 1, 2021. This gives you a strong incentive to file for registration as early as possible. Exceptions to the priority right of use are marks used before your filing date, applications filed before your application, and, in some circumstances, applications filed by foreign applicants.

Assignments

You can assign actual-use applications, but intent-to-use applications can be assigned only to your own business. This prevents people from filing applications for the sole purpose of selling them.

Benefits of Registration

Registering your mark provides many benefits. First, you can use the ® symbol or the phrase "registered trademark" in conjunction with your mark only if it's federally registered. You can, however, use TM for trademark or SM for service mark with an unregistered mark. These designations have no official status, but they notify others that you're claiming a property right in the mark.

Second, registration on the Principal Register is evidence of the validity of the registration, the registrant's ownership of the mark, and the exclusive right to use the mark on identified goods in commerce. Finally, and perhaps most importantly, a registered trademark that has been in continuous use for a period of five consecutive years may become incontestable. By registering the trademark, you can secure rights superior to those of a prior but unregistered user, so long as the first user doesn't object to your use before that five-year period is over.

Duration

Under the trademark law, registration remains in effect for a period of ten years. It may be renewed in additional ten-year increments by filing an application for renewal during the year prior to the expiration of the existing ten-year term.

Supplemental Register

Registration on the Supplemental Register provides protection for marks used in commerce that are distinguishable from those of others but don't meet requirements for registration on the Principal Register. Most often, registrations on the Supplemental Register are for descriptive marks for which the owner hasn't been able to prove secondary meaning. Supplemental Register applications can be made either in response to the USPTO's final refusal to register the mark on the Principal Register or directly. Unless you believe there's no real possibility of registration on the Principal Register, it's best to try to register your mark on the Principal Register, since many more benefits are available for marks registered on the Principal Register.

Marks for the Supplemental Register aren't published for, or subject to, opposition. They are, however, published as registered in the Official Gazette. Those who believe they will be damaged by the registration of a mark on the Supplemental Register can, at any time, petition for cancellation of the registration. Applications filed on the Supplemental Register can't be based on intent-to-use and don't enjoy the benefits of constructive use.

Loss of Protection

A number of well-known trademarks, such as Dry Ice, Thermos, and TV Dinners, have been lost as a result of improper usage. Trademark protection is lost when a mark is used in some capacity other than as an adjective modifying a noun. When a trademark is used as a noun or a verb, it no longer functions to identify the source of the product but becomes the name of the product itself. Because it's now generic, it's no longer protected as a trademark. Abandonment of a mark also results in loss of protection. A trademark is considered abandoned when it hasn't been used for two years and there's no intent to resume its use. You don't have to use the mark in interstate commerce, but you do have to at least use it in intrastate commerce. Token use isn't sufficient to avoid abandonment.

The Trademark Modernization Act of 2020 allows third parties to request expungement of a registration on the grounds that the mark was never used in commerce on or in connection with some or all of the goods or services recited in the registration. Further, reexamination of a registration can be requested on the basis that the mark wasn't in use in commerce on or in connection with some or all of the goods or services recited in the registration on or before use was alleged.

INFRINGEMENT

Assuming you have a valid mark and you're using it in commerce, you can sue an infringer for monetary damages or for an injunction prohibiting the infringing use, or sometimes for both. Monetary damages may be measured either by the plaintiff's losses resulting from the infringement or by the defendant's profits. In certain exceptional circumstances where the defendant's conduct is willful and flagrant, the plaintiff might also be entitled to exemplary damages equal to three times the actual damages and/or attorney's fees. Intent-to-use applicants can't sue for infringement until they actually use the mark.

Antidilution

In the past, it was possible to use a mark on goods or services that don't compete with those of the mark's owner so long as there was no likelihood of confusion, but the federal trademark law was amended in 1996 to provide owners of famous marks with protection from dilution. A famous mark is one that is "widely recognized by the general consuming public of the United States as a designation of source of the goods or services of the mark's owner." The remedies available for violations of the antidilution statute are comparable to those for trademark infringement.

INTERNATIONAL PROTECTION

As of the date of this writing, the United States doesn't belong to any treaty providing international trademark protection. In 2003, the United States became a party to the Madrid Accord, which allows Americans to apply for trademark protection in 123 countries (as of the date of this writing) by filing the appropriate application and paying the required fees to the USPTO. This process is much simpler than applying directly to each country's trademark office and means you won't have to hire a specialist in each country. For a current listing of participating countries, as well as the fees charged and application process, see http://www.wipo.int/madrid.

STATE REGISTRATION

Trademarks can also be registered under state law. State law protection of a trademark doesn't extend beyond the borders of the state but is sometimes broader than that offered by the federal law. The registration fee and rules for specimens vary from state to state.

USING AN ATTORNEY

Trademark registration is beneficial to anyone in the food and beverage industry who has invested time, money, and energy in developing a reputation for quality products and services. Because procuring trademark protection on either the state or federal level requires time and skill, an experienced trademark attorney may prove invaluable. An attorney can, first of all, determine if the benefits to be derived from registration justify the expenses. The total cost of trademark registration usually runs about $1,500 (as of the date of this writing), not counting any artist's fees for drawings.

Second, an attorney can research trademark databases to determine if there are any conflicting marks. Finally, an attorney can complete the application (which is more complex than it appears) and deal with any problems that occur while it's being processed for registration.

Avoid online trademark registration companies, which usually don't employ attorneys licensed to practice in the United States to perform the services. There's a lot more to the process than just obtaining a registration, and handling the entire process properly is critical when seeking registration. Otherwise, the resulting registration might be unenforceable. In fact, we've worked with clients who have discovered in litigation that the registrations they obtained on their own or through online services are invalid. See Chapter 23 for advice on choosing an attorney.

CHAPTER 11

Copyrights

Food and beverage companies commonly use menus, websites, sales literature, apps, software, videos, artwork, music, and other materials designed and created by others. These materials are likely protected by copyright law, in which case your unauthorized use of them could subject you to liability for copyright infringement. In addition, some businesses develop their own copyrightable materials. If you do, you'll probably want to prevent others from using your work without your permission. This chapter discusses some of the many ways the copyright laws may apply to your business.

COPYRIGHT LAW FOUNDATION

Copyright law in the United States has its foundation in the Constitution, which gives Congress the power to "promote the Progress of Science and useful Arts, by securing for limited Times to Authors and Inventors the exclusive Right to their respective Writings and Discoveries." The first Congress enacted a copyright law, and a number of changes to the law have occurred since then. Currently the Copyright Revision Act of 1976, as amended, is the only legislation governing copyright in the United States.

COPYRIGHTABLE MATERIAL

An "author," from the point of view of copyright law, is a creator, such as a photographer, writer, graphic designer, computer programmer, or musician.

An author is granted copyright protection to original works of authorship fixed in any tangible medium of expression.

The law expressly exempts from copyright protection any idea, procedure, process, system, method of operation, concept, principle, or discovery. In short, a copyright extends only to the expression of creations of the mind, not to the ideas themselves. A pure idea, like a plan to create an innovative advertising program for your restaurant, can't be copyrighted—no matter how original or creative that idea is.

A work can be copyrighted only if it's original and shows some creativity. Originality—as distinguished from uniqueness—requires that a work be created independently. It doesn't mean the work is the only one of its kind. If two restaurants coincidentally write long menu descriptions for their gourmet burgers in the exact same language, neither is infringing the other's copyright, and each restaurant can protect its own rights against those who do copy its menu wording. The amount of creativity required is "extremely low," according to the US Supreme Court, and "even a slight amount will suffice." If the "creative spark" is lacking or "so trivial as to be virtually nonexistent," the work isn't protected by copyright.

SCOPE OF PROTECTION

A copyright is actually a collection of five exclusive rights:

- the right to reproduce a work by any means;
- the right to prepare derivative works based on a copyrighted work (a derivative work is one that transforms or adapts the subject matter of one or more preexisting works);
- the right to distribute copies to the public for sale or lease, although once a person sells a copyrighted work or allows uncontrolled distribution of it, the right to control further uses of that work usually ends (this is known as the first sale doctrine, and it doesn't apply to rentals, licenses, or loans);
- the right to perform the work publicly, such as to broadcast a film on YouTube or to show it in a lecture room or meeting room; and
- the right to display the work publicly, though once the copyright owner has sold a copy of the work, the purchaser has the right to display that copy.

These rights are divisible, which means they can be transferred as a whole or separately.

In Plain English

Publication is a technical term that applies to all copyrightable material and means the distribution of copies of a work to the public by sale or other transfer of ownership, or by rental, lease, or loan.

OWNERSHIP

As a general rule, the creator of a work owns the copyright, that is, all the rights mentioned above. Unless there's a written agreement to the contrary, the creator retains the copyright when the work is sold.

Works Made for Hire

Works considered "works made for hire" are an important exception to the general rule that a creator of a work owns the copyright in it. The copyright in a work made by an employee within the scope of employment is owned by the employer, not the employee who created it. This only seems fair, given that the work was produced on behalf of and under the direction of the employer, who paid all the related costs (including payment for the employee's time) and bears all the risks of loss. The parties can, however, avoid the application of this rule with a well-written contract.

Joint Works

The creators of a joint work are co-owners of the copyright in the work, and whatever profit one creator makes from use of the work must be shared equally with the others, unless they have a written agreement that states otherwise. A "joint work" is a work prepared by two or more authors with the intention that their contributions be merged into inseparable or interdependent parts of a unitary whole. The key point is the intent that the parts be absorbed or combined into an integrated unit at the time the work is created. Although this intent must exist at the time the work is created, the authors don't necessarily have to work together, work during the same period, or even know each other.

Independent Contractors

An independent contractor owns the copyright in work created for someone else—even though that person or business was paid for the work's creation—unless there's a written agreement to the contrary (in many jurisdictions, the written contract must predate the performance of the work). Also, the work must have been specially ordered or commissioned as a contribution to a collective work, a supplementary work (one that introduces, revises, comments upon, or assists a work by another), a compilation, an instructional text, answer material for a test or the test itself, an atlas, a motion picture, or an audiovisual work.

In Plain English

If you have a license to use copyrighted work, be careful not to exceed the terms of the license. Get all licenses in writing and make sure they specifically describe the scope of the rights you're being granted. Imagine that you hire an artist as an independent contractor to create an image for your menu covers—can you also use that image on your take-out bags? Unless the agreement says you can, the answer is "no."

Derivative Works

A derivative work is, generally speaking, a work based upon one or more preexisting works. Any work based completely or partially upon a preexisting work is separately copyrightable if it satisfies the originality requirement—so long as it isn't itself an infringing work. The creator of a derivative work owns only what that person contributed.

Collective Works

A collective work is one in which a number of contributions, constituting separate and independent works in themselves, are assembled into a collective whole. Examples include magazines and anthologies. The originality involved in a collective work is the collection and assembling of preexisting works that might themselves be copyrightable, without any changes in that material.

COPYRIGHT PROTECTION FOR UTILITARIAN OBJECTS

The copyright in a design of a useful article is protected "only if, and only to the extent that, such design incorporates pictorial, graphic, or sculptural features that can be identified separately from, and are capable of existing independently of, the utilitarian aspects of the article." In 2017, the US Supreme Court clarified this statute, holding that a feature incorporated into the design of a useful article is eligible for copyright protection only if the feature (1) can be perceived as a two- or three-dimensional work of art separate from the useful article and (2) would qualify as a protectable pictorial, graphic, or sculptural work—either on its own or fixed in some other tangible medium of expression—if it were imagined separately from the useful article it's incorporated into.

If, for instance, you carve ornate designs into the wooden booths at your brewpub, the designs might be protectable, even though the booths themselves are functional. Similarly, designs on your uniforms can be copyrighted even though the uniforms function to cover your staff's bodies, to protect them from the elements and workplace injuries, and to identify them as employees of your business.

NOTICE REQUIREMENT

A copyright notice consists of the international symbol "©" or the word "copyright" or its abbreviation "Copr.", the name of the author (in the case of works for hire, this is usually the employer), and the year of first publication. The order of the words is unimportant. For example, these are both valid notices:

Copyright 2022 by John Doe
or
© Jane Doe, 2022

In the past, publication of a work without notice caused the work to fall into the public domain, but notice isn't required on works created or first published after March 1, 1989. Although it isn't mandatory, you should still use a copyright notice to make others aware of your rights. Someone who copies a work, believing it to be in the public domain because there's no notice, might be considered an innocent infringer. In this situation, the author whose work is copied likely won't recover significant damages, and the court might even allow the copier to continue using the work.

To help prevent claims of innocent infringement, the copyright notice should be placed on the item in such a way that it's permanently legible to any ordinary user of the work.

APPLICATION PROCESS

To register a copyright, you must file an application form with the Copyright Office. You can file online at www.copyright.gov or file a paper form. As of this writing, the online application fee is $45 to $65, while the paper application fee is $125. Depending on the type of work and how the application is filed, you must also deposit one or two copies of the work. While the application might seem simple enough for you to fill out on your own, have an intellectual property attorney assist you the first time you do so, because the application is significantly more complicated than it first appears.

Remember, if you have a copyright notice on your work, or if your work was published after March 1, 1989, even without a notice, you probably already have a copyright. Under the current law, registration is necessary only:

- if you want to sue for infringement;
- if you want to effectively protect your work under the Digital Millennium Copyright Act (DMCA), which, among other things, has a takedown procedure for infringing content on the Internet; or
- if the Register of Copyrights demands registration of a published work bearing a copyright notice (which isn't likely to happen).

You may have heard about the so-called "poor person's copyright," the practice of mailing a copy of your own work to yourself. In reality, this doesn't give you any more copyright protection than you already have, and it isn't a substitute for registration.

Delaying Registration

Although you can delay registration, there are many reasons you should deposit the work and file an application for registration within three months of publication. For one thing, you can't enforce your copyright until you've done so, because you can't bring a lawsuit for copyright infringement until you apply for and receive either a certificate of registration or a denial of registration from the Copyright Office. Also, if you send a takedown notice under the DMCA demanding removal of infringing content and the person who posted the material sends a counter-notification, you have only ten to fourteen days to file a lawsuit, or the infringing material will be put back up on the website. In reality, then, you can't count on DMCA takedowns unless you've already registered the copyright.

One of the most important reasons to register your copyrights promptly is that you aren't eligible for an award of attorney's fees and statutory damages for infringements that occur before registration unless you registered the work's copyright within three months of publication. Also, if you register your copyright within five years after first publication of the work, the registration constitutes prima facie evidence (a rebuttable presumption) of the validity of the copyright and of the facts stated in the certificate of registration.

PERIOD OF PROTECTION

Works created on or after January 1, 1978, generally have copyright protection from the instant they're fixed in tangible form until 70 years after the creator's death. If the work was created jointly, the copyright expires 70 years after the last author dies. The copyright period of life plus 70 years applies only to works created by human beings using their own names. In other cases (e.g., works made for hire and works created anonymously or pseudonymously), the period of protection is either 120 years from creation or 95 years from first publication, whichever expires first.

INFRINGEMENT

The statute of limitations allows a plaintiff three years to file a lawsuit after the infringement occurs, meaning the date the infringement was committed, not the date the infringement was discovered. The federal courts have exclusive jurisdiction over copyright infringement litigation. If you successfully prove infringement, you might be awarded the actual damages you suffered as well as any profits of the infringer attributable to the infringement that weren't considered in computing the actual damages.

If the copyright was timely registered, you can choose an award of statutory damages instead. Statutory damages may be as little as $200 for innocent infringement, between $750 and $30,000 for the typical case, and up to $150,000 for willful infringement. In the case of willful infringement for commercial gain, criminal sanctions may also be imposed. The court can, in its discretion, award reasonable attorneys' fees to the prevailing party, whether that's the plaintiff or the defendant, though the plaintiff is eligible for an attorneys' fee award only if registration was timely made. The court can also issue an injunction against continued infringement and impoundment of infringing items.

The Copyright Alternative in Small-Claims Enforcement (CASE) Act of 2020 creates a Copyright Claims Board within the US Copyright Office. This board, which will be similar to a small claims court, will hear claims of copyright infringement and abuses of the DMCA takedown procedures as well as actions for declarations of noninfringement. The proceedings will be more streamlined than in federal court, and damages are capped at $15,000 per claim or $30,000 for all claims, not including any attorneys' fees and costs that may be awarded. Up to $5,000 in attorneys' fees may be awarded upon a showing of bad faith conduct, with higher awards possible in "extraordinary" circumstances.

NONINFRINGING USES

Not every copying of a protected work is an infringement. There are two basic types of noninfringing use—fair use and exempted use.

Fair Use

Copies of a protected work for purposes of criticism, comment, news reporting, teaching (including multiple copies for classroom use), scholarship, or research can be considered fair use and, therefore, not an infringement. However, this isn't a complete list; nor is it intended as a definition of fair use. The copyright statute cites four criteria to be considered in determining whether a particular use is or isn't fair:

- the purpose and character of the use, including whether it's for commercial use or nonprofit educational purposes;
- the nature of the copyrighted work;

- the amount and substantiality of the portion used in relation to the copyrighted work as a whole; and
- the effect of the use upon the potential market for, or value of, the copyrighted work.

These four criteria aren't ranked, and other factors can be considered as well.

You might have heard that changing a work by a certain percentage or copying only a certain percentage of a work automatically means your work is fair use, but that's not true. In some cases, copyright infringement is found when only a very small part of a work has been copied; in other situations, a much larger part can be copied without infringing.

Exemptions

Exemptions apply in situations where the public interest in making copies outweighs the potential harm to the copyright proprietor. For example, the library and archives exemption allows libraries and archives to reproduce and distribute a single copy of a work so long as certain requirements are met.

INTERNATIONAL PROTECTION

The United States is a party to three multinational copyright treaties. The Buenos Aires Convention, in effect in the Western Hemisphere, provides international protection within member countries if the words "all rights reserved" are added to the copyright notice. The United States is also a party to the Universal Copyright Convention, which requires a copyright owner to use the international copyright symbol "Ó" as part of the copyright notice. The oldest multinational copyright treaty is the Berne Copyright Convention, though the United States didn't become a party to it until 1989. This treaty mandates the relaxation of copyright formalities and requires greater protection be afforded copyright owners.

For a list of the countries that are parties to these treaties and have reciprocal rights with the United States, see www.copyright.gov. The protection afforded copyright owners under these treaties is automatic so long as the minimal compliance standards are met. In this respect, international protection of copyrights is more available than international protection of other forms of intellectual property.

CHAPTER 12

Advertising

When creating an advertising program for your food or beverage business, you should work with an attorney skilled in advertising law in order to be assured of having an effective program that doesn't expose your business to potential liability. A poorly planned advertising program is likely to be more harmful than not having any advertising at all. This chapter covers several important legal considerations that might arise when planning an advertising program.

GOVERNMENT REGULATION

General Regulations

A business can always tout the qualities of its products or services, but those representations must be true. Most states have consumer protection laws that, among other things, impose fines and other legal sanctions on businesses that engage in misleading advertising. The state attorney general can cause an offending advertisement to be withdrawn and may even require corrective advertising.

Similarly, the Federal Trade Commission (FTC) polices businesses that are engaged in interstate commerce. If your business activity extends beyond your state boundaries and affects another state, then the FTC has jurisdiction over your company. This is also true if you advertise over the web. In fact, your online advertising might be subject to regulation throughout the world, which is especially problematic since the laws of other countries are often quite different than those in the United States.

Industry-Specific Regulations

In addition to the regulations that apply to all businesses, some laws and regulations apply specifically to businesses in the food and beverage industry. For instance, the marketing of alcoholic beverages is tightly regulated, and all health claims you make about food and beverages must be substantiated. Truth-in-Menu laws protect consumers from fraud by food-service operators. The menu must accurately reflect the price the customer will be charged, and any mandatory service, cover, or minimum charges must be clearly disclosed. All statements about preparation style, ingredients, origin, portion sizes, and health benefits must be accurate.

This means the food you serve must match the menu's description—a hamburger advertised as containing half a pound of beef must contain eight ounces of beef. If a geographic source for the food is given ("Maine lobster"), the food must, in fact, be from that geographic area. Also, if a food is advertised as "grilled," it must, in fact, be grilled. Food manufactured with "grill marks" doesn't meet legal requirements. Likewise, "homemade" products must be made on-site. Contact an attorney knowledgeable in this area if you have any questions about your menu. Federal regulations also require restaurants to provide customers on request data to back up claims regarding nutrition or health. Examples include "high in omega 3 fatty acids" and "heart healthy." If you make any claims like this, it would be wise to have them reviewed by a dietitian.

Make sure your claims aren't misleading, even if technically true. In a 2018 case, the US Court of Appeals for the Second Circuit ruled that labeling crackers "made with whole grain" when they were made mostly of white flour could mislead consumers. On the other hand, a California court found that "milk from grass-fed cows" in a promotion for butter didn't imply that the cows never ate anything else. Because this area of law is more complex than it might appear, it's a good idea to have all of your claims reviewed by an experienced attorney.

COMPARATIVE ADVERTISING

Businesses often promote the merits of their products and services by comparing them with those of their competitors. Comparative advertising is legal in the United States so long as the statements are true, and there's no likelihood that a consumer would believe the advertiser is also selling the competing product or service.

For example, a restaurant named Blue Strawberry might claim that its burgers are better than those of its competitor, Pink Blueberry. Blue Strawberry can, if accurate, also advertise that Pink Blueberry's patties include textured vegetable protein, whereas Blue Strawberry's patties are 100 percent ground beef. If, however, Pink Blueberry has 100 percent beef patties, then Blue Strawberry may be liable to Pink Blueberry for making the false statement.

For a disparaging remark to be unlawful, it must be both untrue and believable by a reasonable person. If the statement made was so outlandish as to be unbelievable, it's unlikely the owner whose product was disparaged will be able to prove any injury. If, for example, a restaurant claims that its competitors' ice cream is made out of penguin snot, the likelihood is that no one would believe this gross (no pun intended) exaggeration.

What about implied comparisons? While such a comparison could be problematic, in 2020 a California court held that labeling fruit juice "no sugar added" didn't imply that all competing products have added sugar. In fact, some other juices have added sugar, and some don't.

PUBLICITY AND PRIVACY

You can use a celebrity to endorse your products and services, but only if the celebrity consents. If not, you might be liable for violating the celebrity's right of publicity. This right is granted by the majority of states in the United States to those who commercially exploit their names, voices, or images, such as sports figures, actors, or singers. The use of a look-alike for commercial purposes may also be actionable. For example, liability was imposed on manufacturers who used look-alikes for Jackie Onassis, Woody Allen, and rap group the Fat Boys.

People who haven't achieved notoriety because of their commercial activities have a right of privacy, which means they have a claim if their names or likenesses are used in an advertisement without their permission. This applies even to your own employees, so get written permission before using their names, voices, or likenesses for advertising purposes.

If an individual's photograph isn't the focal point of the ad, but is merely an incidental part, such as a head in a crowd, then that person's permission might not be essential for the photograph to be used commercially. Even when you're not required to have permission before using someone's photograph, it's still a good idea to get a signed photo release if possible. Word the release in a way that gives your business permission to use the name and likeness or, where relevant, the person's voice, for any and all purposes, including advertising your business. This will protect you if, for example, that person later becomes famous and you want to continue to use their photo in your advertisements.

UNAUTHORIZED USE OF TRADEMARK

You're generally allowed to use the name or logo of another business in your advertisement as long as there's no likelihood that an average person would believe the ad was sponsored by the other company. For instance, you might have an ad containing a photo of a patron in your restaurant holding a copyrighted publication like *USA Today*, or an automobile commercial might show the advertised vehicle cruising past your restaurant's sign bearing its registered trademark.

TRADE DRESS

A form of advertising that has been given special protection is package design. While it's true that the copyright laws don't protect functional items like product packaging, the courts have developed a form of protection known as trade dress. This means that the design elements of a particular packaging design are protectable so long as they're not otherwise functional. Trade dress has been extended beyond traditional packaging. In 1992, the US Supreme Court endorsed the expansion of the doctrine in *Two Pesos v. Taco Cabana*, ruling that a restaurant's architectural features, décor, and menu can be protected so long as they have a distinctive look and feel, aren't functional, and have achieved notoriety. For instance, IHOP's blue A-shaped roof is a protected trade dress.

In 2000, the US Supreme Court clarified the trade dress doctrine, holding that someone claiming that the trade dress in their unregistered product design has been infringed must prove that the alleged trade dress is distinctive with an extensive survey of consumers showing that they recognize the unique look and feel of the item involved. As of this writing, the court hasn't applied the same requirement to package-design trade dress.

The First Amendment allows some uses of trade dress belonging to someone else. For example, in 2020, a federal appellate court held that the parody chew toys for dogs at issue in the case were expressive works entitled to First Amendment protection. Although the Jack Daniel's trade dress and bottle design were used to sell the "Bad Spaniel" toys, the court believed they were intended to convey a humorous message.

In Plain English

Many businesses have begun to register their trade dress. This is accomplished by registering the distinctive look and feel as a trademark (trademark registration is discussed in Chapter 10). Registration means the trade dress is presumed valid under federal trademark law. Examples of registered trade dress are the distinctive shape of a Coca-Cola bottle and the McDonald's golden arches.

Celebrity Trade Dress

Individuals can also have distinctive styles. For example, when an advertiser hired one of Bette Midler's backup singers to replicate Ms. Midler's distinctive vocal rendition of a song for a commercial, Ms. Midler sued and recovered for the knockoff. The California statute protects, among other things, a celebrity's voice. When, however, a manufacturer hired a group that looked and sounded like the group known as the Fat Boys, the federal court in New York held the manufacturer liable only for violating the celebrities' publicity rights. The court refused to impose liability for the unauthorized use of the Fat Boys' sound since the New York publicity statute extends protection merely to one's name, portrait, or picture, and not to one's sound.

GEOGRAPHIC LOCATIONS

Geographic locations can usually be used in advertisements without obtaining the owner's consent, so you could advertise your pinot gris by having someone stand in front of a famous building, such as the Empire State Building. This is because items of utility aren't copyrightable. Buildings, parks, and other landmarks can be used in advertising programs without the owner's permission. However, one case held that a building that was architecturally unique, identifiable, and famous could enjoy the protection of the trade dress laws when it was prominently featured on a poster.

ENDORSEMENTS

The FTC has issued guidelines requiring bloggers, social network site users, and others who create online product reviews to disclose the receipt of free merchandise or payment for those reviews. Companies who pay for reviews or who give those reviewers free products or services can, under some circumstances, be held liable for false or unsubstantiated statements made through endorsements or for failing to disclose any "material connection" between themselves and their endorsers.

Advertisers have an obligation to monitor endorsers and to advise them of their obligations under the guidelines. You should, therefore, provide your own guidelines to bloggers and other third parties endorsing your products or services when you offer them payments or discounted products or services. If, for instance, your restaurant offers a food blogger a free meal, be sure to remind the blogger of the need to disclose the free meal when writing about your restaurant.

When writing your guidelines, cover the obligations of the blogger (or other endorser) to make only truthful and substantiated claims about your product or service and to clearly disclose any "material connection" (e.g., free product, payments, employment of the reviewer by the advertiser). Also, create programs for monitoring the statements made by these endorsers and implement internal policies prohibiting your employees from writing reviews about your company's products or services.

The FTC guidelines cover reviews posted on sites like Amazon, so although there are plenty of unscrupulous people out there willing to post fake "verified purchase" reviews in exchange for payment, you should avoid this type of arrangement when you sell your food and beverage products online. The FTC has begun to focus more on enforcement of these guidelines, especially as they relate to fake reviews.

Celebrity Endorsements

Under FTC guidelines, celebrity endorsers and the advertisers who hire them can be held liable for false or unsubstantiated claims that the endorsers make. You can no longer pay celebrities to say whatever you want them to about your product or service. Rather, their statements must reflect their own "honest opinions, findings, beliefs, or experience." The celebrity can't simply read from a script but will need to have actually used the product or service being endorsed. Also, the statements must be only those that are, in the celebrity's own experience, accurate. This means if you want a celebrity to talk about how great your restaurant's tacos are, you must ensure the celebrity not only tries your tacos but likes them.

Celebrities are also required to disclose their relationships with advertisers when making endorsements outside the context of traditional advertisements. That is, a celebrity promoting a product such as your hazy IPA on a social networking site (e.g., Instagram, Facebook, or Twitter) or on a talk show must disclose any payment or other arrangement relating to that product or service.

Research

If your business sponsors a research organization to study a product, and the study is used to promote the product in an ad, the ad must, in accordance with FTC guidelines, disclose the connection between the advertiser and the research organization. For example, if you pay for a study showing that your kimchi's probiotics help with anxiety, you'll need to disclose that payment.

"Typical" Results

FTC guidelines also require that advertisements featuring a consumer and conveying an experience with a product or service as "typical" when that isn't true must clearly disclose what consumers should generally expect. Earlier guidelines allowed advertisers to describe the consumer's experience as long as they included a "results not typical" disclaimer. This is a frequent issue in the advertisement of "diet" foods and weight loss products.

Social Media Influencers

Social media influencers are those with dedicated groups of followers viewed as experts within their niche. When these influencers recommend specific brands, their followers tend to trust their advice. In other words, an ardent follower of a local food-porn Instagrammer who sees a post touting your bakery is likely to visit your bakery. For this reason, FTC guidelines require an influencer to properly disclose any financial, personal, family, or employment relationship to a brand.

The reasoning is obvious. Customers might not be as eager to visit the bakery hashtagged in the croissant photo when they find out the Instagrammer was paid by your bakery or that your bakery happens to be owned by the Instagrammer's sister. Of course, this is precisely why businesses and social media influencers prefer not to disclose their relationship: an endorsement is more effective if an influencer's followers believe the endorsement is an honest evaluation based on the influencer's personal experience and knowledge.

You could be liable for an influencer's failure to make proper disclosures, so institute a policy for your influencers requiring them to disclose all financial, personal, family, and employment relationships with your business. Disclosures must be hard to miss and in clear, simple language.

CHAPTER 13

Intellectual Property Licenses

Most food and beverage businesses use some form of intellectual property in connection with their operations. It's important for you to properly protect your rights so you can use them yourself as well as expand your financial opportunities by licensing others to use your rights for a fee. You'll probably also obtain licenses to use others' intellectual property, like software and music.

WHAT IS A LICENSE?

In short, a license is permission. For example, your brewpub's liquor license is permission for it to sell alcohol. This chapter is about licenses—or permissions—to use intellectual property rights. An intellectual property license is an arrangement between an intellectual property rights owner (the licensor) and somebody who's being authorized to use those rights (the licensee). The licensor retains ownership of its intellectual property but gives the licensee permission to use the specified intellectual property rights in specific ways and for a specific amount of time in exchange for a fee or royalty.

LICENSING YOUR INTELLECTUAL PROPERTY

A license to use your copyright, trademark, trade dress, or patent should be in writing. Make sure it describes the scope of the user's permission, such as how long the license will last, whether the user can market the licensed product or service throughout the world or only in specific locations, and whether the license allows exploitation of the entire intellectual property or only a portion of it. For instance, you might allow the licensee to use your restaurant's trademark on bottles of hot sauce made using your recipe, but not on any other merchandise.

Trademarks

When licensing an unaffiliated commercial kitchen to produce your hot sauce as described in the example above, you'll need to establish and enforce quality control guidelines. Not only can licensing without appropriate quality control damage your business's reputation, but if you license a trademark without establishing and enforcing quality control standards, the license might be considered a "naked license," resulting in the invalidation of your trademark. You'll also need to require the licensee to use the appropriate notice, ® or TM. Always work with an experienced intellectual-property lawyer when licensing your trademark.

Patented Technology

If you're considering licensing a patented technology, for instance, a new type of fermentation vessel, the safety of the technology and potential for liability arising from its use should be evaluated. Licenses can be drafted with exculpatory clauses in which the licensee agrees to assume all liability arising from its use of the licensed technology, although these clauses may not entirely insulate the licensor from liability. Careful testing of the technology to ensure removal of defects will reduce the risk of liability as well.

Trade Secrets

A restaurant's signature dishes and the distinct characteristics of the food served in the restaurant are likely what establish its position in the marketplace. Similarly, craft brewers, winemakers, and others in the food and beverage industry have their own signature recipes and styles. As discussed in Chapter 9, recipes can be protected as trade secrets, so licensing their use is possible—though it's usually best for your business's recipes and style to be sold only under its trademarks. You might, however, license your trade secrets in connection with your trademark, as in the hot sauce example above. You must make sure that trade secrets are protected by using an appropriate nondisclosure agreement with the licensee.

Copyrights

Most food and beverage businesses won't be licensing copyrights, but if your business is, make sure you provide the licensee with the appropriate copyright notice. Remember too that you can separately license the individual rights that make up a copyright (see Chapter 11 for a description of those rights).

License Agreements

Lawyers who specialize in intellectual property can explain the numerous possibilities available to you through the licensing process and can draft an agreement to afford you maximum protection. A skilled lawyer can also determine whether the licensing arrangement you're proposing is subject to franchising laws (see Chapter 8). Whenever possible, record your license in the appropriate place—the Copyright Office or the US Patent and Trademark Office (USPTO). An intellectual property lawyer can assist you with this process.

In Plain English

Licensing is so important that entire trade shows are devoted to this field. One of the most prominent is the Licensing Expo held in May at the Mandalay Bay Convention Center in Las Vegas. For more information, check its website at www.licensingexpo.com.

LICENSING OTHERS' INTELLECTUAL PROPERTY

Virtually every food and beverage business needs to license intellectual property from others. Two of the most common types of licenses are those for software and music, though items such as photographs and graphic designs are often licensed—not sold—by the artist. Often you can negotiate a purchase of all rights of items designed specifically for your business in exchange for payment of a higher fee. If it's too late for that, carefully review the fine print of your invoice or contract to see just what you have the right to do with any those items.

If, for example, you hire someone to photograph your offerings for your menu, you might be surprised to learn that you can't use the photos on your website. Unless you work something else out with the photographer, the photographer will likely retain the copyright and you'll find you only have the right to use those photos in your menu. Similarly, if you have a graphic designer create an image to be used on T-shirts worn by your tasting room staff, you might not be allowed to use that image on souvenir wineglasses.

Software

Software is licensed to its users with numerous restrictions. Software audits are regularly conducted to determine whether businesses have appropriate licenses for the software on their systems and are complying with the software licenses they do have. Some of the most common license infractions include making more copies of a program than allowed, using the less-expensive academic or home version of a program in your business, allowing more people to use a program than the licenses permit, and installing a program with a single license on more than one computer.

Software audits may be conducted directly by software vendors or by alliances of vendors, such as the Business Software Alliance (BSA) and the Software & Information Industry Association (SIIA). As you might expect, most of these audits end with the software vendor claiming the customer doesn't have the appropriate licenses and demanding payment of significant damages and reimbursement of attorneys' fees, as well as the purchase of additional licenses. Plus, the auditor customarily requires ongoing monitoring, which can be even more expensive and time-consuming.

Always read and comply with software licenses. If you have employees, notify them in writing that pirating software is prohibited, and set up computers so that most employees can't install software. Buy software from a reputable source and save all software records, including receipts and licenses, so that you'll be able to show compliance if you're audited. Also, conduct regular internal audits to make sure all software on company electronic devices is properly licensed and that your records are current.

Music, Radio, and Television

While there are some limited exceptions allowing you to play radio and television if you don't charge patrons to listen (in other words, they don't have to pay a cover charge) and meet the other requirements, everything else must be licensed regardless of your business's size. You can obtain a "blanket" public performance license for all the music represented by a performance rights organization (PRO). Licenses fees are generally paid yearly and vary depending on a variety of factors, such as whether the music is live or recorded, whether you impose a cover charge, the square footage of your location, and its customer capacity.

Payment to a PRO like the American Society of Composers, Authors and Publishers (ASCAP), Broadcast Music, Inc. (BMI), SESAC (previously the Society of European Stage Authors and Composers) or Global Music Rights (GMR) covers all fees due to the composers, artists, and publishers represented by that particular PRO. This means you may need to acquire licenses from all of the PROs. You must strictly comply with the copyright laws and the terms of any licenses you obtain, because representatives of the PROs visit bars, restaurants, and other establishments, posing as customers, and then check to see if you have appropriate licenses for the music you've played.

If you hire musicians to play live music, you're responsible for ensuring that all music played is properly licensed. Although both your business and the musicians will be liable for copyright infringement if the license isn't acquired, the industry standard is for venues to obtain the necessary public performance licenses. Buying a CD or MP3, streaming music from a service like Spotify or Pandora (even if you use the paid version), or playing the radio doesn't mean you can skip paying for a license from one or more PROs, because you still need a license to play the music in public.

Similarly, unless you qualify for an exemption, you must obtain a performance license for audiovisual content. Most cable and satellite TV providers offer special packages for businesses like restaurants and bars that cover the rights to the programming, but you'll need to carefully review what's covered. For example, the package might not cover the music licenses for music that appears in programs, and you might have to obtain your own licenses from the PROs.

And just as buying a CD doesn't allow you to play it publicly, purchasing a DVD doesn't allow you to play the movie or TV show publicly. Nor can you simply stream the videos from the Internet, even if you're using a paid service like Netflix or Hulu. Always get the required licenses before publicly showing any video. There are companies similar to the PROs described above that license movies and, in some cases, television shows. These include MPLC, Swank Motion Pictures, Inc., and Criterion Pictures, USA.

Because commercial accounts and licensing fees are expensive, you might think using a residential account for your business is a good way to save money—after all, what are the odds of you getting caught? Probably a lot higher than you think. Music, radio, and TV providers hire investigators to find violators by visiting bars and restaurants. This is especially common in the pay-per-view industry.

If a provider learns that you don't have the right package for your business, not only may you be liable for breach of contract and copyright infringement, but you might also be violating federal laws applicable to radio, cable, and satellite transmissions. These laws provide that the distributor can recover damages (actual or statutory) and attorneys' fees. Double-check that your business has all necessary licenses and pays the proper commercial rate, because you're liable for breaking these laws even if you do so by accident.

CHAPTER 14

The Internet

Recent studies have found that nearly 90 percent of guests research a restaurant online before dining—more than any other business type—and that 70 percent want the ability to order takeout and delivery online. This statistic was derived before the COVID-19 pandemic, when many states limited restaurants to take-out orders, and an online presence became even more important. Similarly, people looking for caterers, local craft beer and spirits, wine, and gourmet food are likely to begin their search online. For this reason, you'll likely want your business to have a website as well as a strong social media presence.

PROTECTING CONSUMER INFORMATION

A number of laws affect how you handle the consumer information your website collects. A federal law, the Children's Online Privacy Protection Act (COPPA), regulates how websites can collect and use information from and about children under the age of thirteen. Although there's been a push for a broader federal online privacy law, as of this writing, no such law has been enacted. However, a number of privacy laws, such as those requiring a website operator to permit users to "opt out" of the sale of their personal information, have been enacted on the state level, which makes for a confusing patchwork of privacy laws.

In addition, California has adopted legislation requiring certain companies "doing business in California," which includes selling goods or services to California residents (even if the business isn't physically located in

California) to disclose to consumers upon request the categories and specific pieces of personal information that the business has collected, as well as the source of that information and the business purpose for collecting the information. A consumer can also ask a company doing business in California to delete any personal information that the business has collected from that consumer.

DOMAIN NAMES

Characterization of website names has also presented some vexing problems. Is a domain name merely an address (Uniform Resource Locator [URL]) used to locate the site? Or is it a trademark? See Chapter 10 for more information about when URLs are treated as trademarks. The problem is compounded by the fact that most businesses want the ".com" version of their names or trademarks as their URL, but it might not be available because somebody doing business in a different industry or geographical location already has that URL. Competition for domain name registration is fierce, and prices for securing an easy-to-remember domain name are competitive.

Initially, there were five top-level domain name categories for US-based registrants: .com for commerce; .org for organizations; .gov for government; .mil for military; and .edu for educational institutions. As the availability of popular domain names shrank, more than a thousand new URLs became available with new suffixes. These include many of interest to those in the food and beverage business, including .bar, .beer, .cafe, .catering, .coffee, .eat, .pizza, .pub, .restaurant, .vodka, and .wine. URLs with the .com suffix are still the most popular, though.

Disputes

Methods for resolving domain name disputes include litigation in federal district court and the less-expensive online arbitration process using the procedure established by ICANN (the Internet Corporation for Assigned Names and Numbers, www.icann.org.). Anti-cybersquatting legislation is intended to prevent cybersquatters from obtaining domain name registrations for the purpose of reselling them to those who own the trademarks used in those URLs. You should consult a lawyer specializing in online intellectual property issues when these issues arise.

TRADEMARKS

Often, obtaining a trademark registration for your business name provides you with leverage in obtaining and keeping your business name as a domain name. For example, Orange Orca Brews would likely have success in either obtaining the URL orangeorca.com from a cybersquatter or defending that URL against another potential registrant of that domain name if it has registered Orange Orca with the US Patent & Trademark Office (USPTO). As we mentioned in Chapter 10, it's possible to register trademarks through the USPTO in more than a hundred countries throughout the world pursuant to the Madrid Protocol.

COPYRIGHT

Despite what you may hear, you don't have the right to simply copy photos, text, and other materials from another website. These items are generally protected by copyright. Some creators use Creative Commons licenses to allow others to use their works without pay (usually these licenses do require proper attribution), but not all of these licenses permit commercial use or modification of the work. As of this writing, the Creative Commons search function allows you to limit your search by checking boxes for "Use commercially" and "Modify or adapt."

Linking

Early in the history of the Internet, it wasn't clear whether hyperlinks infringed the rights of the owner of the website being linked to. Today, linking to the front page or "deep linking" to a subpage of another website isn't an infringement, so long as the material you're linking to doesn't infringe. The law isn't yet settled on when linking to infringing material might itself be an infringement.

Framing and Embedding

Instead of taking a website user to a linked website, "framing" displays the information from the second website in a special frame associated with the first website. Somewhat confusingly to non-techies, the information isn't actually copied. Rather, the website doing the framing is using HTML code pointing to the information. "Embedding" (also known as "inline linking") is incorporating a graphics or video file from one website into another website. Case law conflicts as to whether framing and embedding are infringing, so to be safe, it's best to avoid these practices unless you have permission from the owner of the content and follow any restrictions imposed in connection with that permission.

INTERNET ADVERTISING

Ads in traditional advertising forums (e.g., magazines, newspapers, radio, and television) are intended to affect conduct in the future. Advertisers typically hope consumers will buy the advertised product or service next time they go shopping (though of course there are occasional ads advising consumers to "Call now!"). Internet shoppers, on the other hand, can instantaneously make a purchase. Another advantage is that Internet ads can be easily targeted to potential buyers. While some of this can happen by advertising during certain shows (for example, if your target audience is foodies, you might advertise during *Top Chef* or in *Food & Wine*), the Internet allows for far more specific targeting. A person who looks up information about hazy IPAs, for instance, will probably be bombarded with ads for that style of beer.

Key Words

One of the more controversial practices is the sale by search engines, like Google, of the right to use a competitor's name or brand to deflect business from the competitor to the purchaser of the ad. The law is still unsettled as to the legality of this practice.

Federal Trade Commission

The Federal Trade Commission ("FTC") enforces a number of requirements for advertisers, social media users, and website operators, ranging from disclosures for websites that attract children to rules for endorsers and social media influencers. Some of these are discussed in Chapter 12, Advertising.

INTERNET AUDITS

An attorney who has expertise in working with websites can conduct an audit of your business's websites, social media accounts, and the like. An Internet audit includes determining whether you have the appropriate permissions to display material (for example, photos), whether trademarks (yours and those of others) are used properly, and whether posted reviews comply with FTC guidelines. Your attorney can also help you draft privacy policies, as well as terms and conditions, for your website or app.

INTERNATIONAL CONCERNS

Since websites are, by definition, worldwide, it's important to determine whether your site could subject you to liability elsewhere, even if it's legal in the United States. For instance, as we mentioned in Chapter 12, while comparative advertising is permissible in the United States, some countries are far more restrictive. Another example is the General Data Protection Regulation (GDPR), which strictly regulates the processing and distribution of the private data of residents of the European Union and the European Economic Area.

You should also be aware that your material may find its way into jurisdictions that don't have copyright treaty relations with the United States. In this event, you might find that you've lost control of your previously protected work. While the World Intellectual Property Organization (WIPO) has expanded the extent of protection available for digital intellectual property with the WIPO Copyright Treaty of 1996, not all countries have adopted or implemented it. As of the date of this writing, there are only 110 parties to the treaty, compared to 179 signatories to the Berne Convention and 193 members of WIPO. Even where the treaty is in force, there's still some risk since it's limited in scope.

THE AMERICANS WITH DISABILITIES ACT

A number of federal courts have ruled that websites are "places" of business under Title III of the Americans with Disabilities Act (ADA), just like restaurants, stores, and movie theaters. One of these cases involved Domino's Pizza. The Ninth Circuit held that even though the Department of Justice hasn't yet issued accessibility guidelines, the website and app for Domino's Pizza are subject to the ADA. This means that you should be sure your website design can accommodate people with disabilities.

Although this area of the law is unsettled, the Web Content Accessibility Guidelines (WCAG) are a blueprint for digital accessibility. Among other things, the WCAG suggest content be presented in different ways, that there be text alternatives for non-text content such as photographs and videos, and that content be made easier for users to hear and see. For more information, see www.w3.org/WAI/standards-guidelines/wcag.

CYBERATTACKS

Whether you host your own website, store programs and data on your own servers, or use cloud-based programs and data storage, you need to guard against cyberattacks to protect your business's trade secrets, as well as the financial information of both your business and your customers. Some types of attacks may even make it impossible for you to continue operating your business.

Be on guard against hacking and phishing attacks, as well as malware. Malware is software that was written with the intent of damaging devices, stealing data, obtaining money, and otherwise creating major headaches for the owners and operators of computers and other devices. Malware includes viruses, Trojans, spyware, ransomware, rootkits, and worms. Consult with a cybersecurity expert in order to take advantage of the latest technology. Don't forget that digital copiers, printers, fax machines, smartphones, tablets, and many other devices are computers and need security as well.

EMAIL

Employee handbooks and policy statements should deal with the proper use of email and intranets as well as other related computer issues. Warn employees that you may monitor their communications and that all other policies (e.g., anti-harassment policies) apply to their email and other online communications.

Spam

The CAN-SPAM Act establishes legal requirements for commercial messages, gives recipients the right to have you stop emailing them, and provides penalties for violations. This law covers all commercial messages, defined as "any electronic mail message the primary purpose of which is the commercial advertisement or promotion of a commercial product or service," including email that promotes content on commercial websites. Your "From," "To,"

"Reply-To," and routing information must be accurate and identify the person or business who sent the message, and your subject line must accurately reflect the content of the message. You also need to identify the message as an ad, include your valid physical postal address, and tell recipients how to opt out of receiving future email from you.

Many states have their own anti-spam laws as well. Interestingly enough, the very word "spam," which has been used to describe bulk email, usually advertising, itself became the subject of litigation. Hormel, the meat company that first developed the name Spam for its canned meat, unsuccessfully sued software companies for using the word as part of the name of their spam-filtering products.

"Reply-To," and routing information must be accurate and identify the person or business who sent the message, and your subject line must accurately reflect the content of the message. You also need to identify the message as an ad, include your valid physical postal address, and tell recipients how to opt out of receiving future email from you.

Many states have their own anti-spam laws as well. Interestingly enough, the very word "spam," which has been used to describe bulk email, usually advertising, itself became the subject of litigation. Hormel, the meat company that first developed the name Spam for its canned meat, unsuccessfully sued software companies for using the word as part of the name of their spam-filtering products.

CHAPTER 15

Warranties

A warranty is, in essence, a guarantee that an item will be of a certain quality or have particular attributes. The rules that govern warranties for products are set forth in the Uniform Commercial Code (UCC), some form of which has been adopted in every state. Giving a warranty involves certain obligations, so you should be aware of what those obligations are, especially since you might be warranting attributes of your business's products or services without realizing it. You'll also want to know what remedies you may have against a vendor who breaches its warranties to you.

EXPRESS WARRANTIES

Any statement of fact or promise that describes the characteristics of an item creates an express warranty. In general, you don't need to use the word "warranty" or "guarantee" to create an express warranty, but the more explicit your statement, the more likely it is that you've given an express warranty. To determine whether a statement gives rise to an express warranty—as opposed to just expressing an opinion—the courts have developed a test. If the seller makes a statement to the buyer relating to goods about which the buyer is uninformed, that statement is probably an express warranty. On the other hand, if the seller merely expresses a judgment about something each party is expected to have an opinion about, no express warranty is given.

If, for example, a manufacturer tells a restaurant owner that a ceramic serving bowl is oven-safe, this statement would likely be considered an express warranty since most buyers—even restaurant owners—don't know much about pottery, and only the seller would know about this bowl in particular. On the other hand, if the manufacturer says the bowl is a good size for soup, it probably won't be considered an express warranty, because the restaurant owner should be able to determine the best size for its own soup bowls.

Making an Express Warranty

When determining whether a statement is an express warranty, a number of factors are relevant. A written statement, particularly if it's part of a contract or bill of sale, is more likely to be considered an express warranty than an oral statement. How much the seller qualifies the statement is also an indication of whether an express warranty is created.

Basis of the Bargain

Another way an express warranty can be created is by giving a description of the item that becomes part of the "basis of the bargain." The description doesn't need to be the only inducement to buy the goods in order for it to constitute a warranty. If a contract is involved, any statements must have been part of the contract negotiations. The precise time a statement is made is irrelevant. The buyer could already have paid for an item and the seller could still make a statement that could be considered part of the basis of the bargain, because the buyer could decide to return the goods for a refund.

This could apply, for example, if your restaurant is purchasing a new wok range and just after you complete the order, you say "This range is ready for use with liquid propane, right?" If the sales representative says "Yes," and it turns out that you have to purchase a conversion kit, you may have a claim for breach of warranty, if you would have immediately changed your order to a different model had you known the truth. These post-purchase statements must, however, be made within a reasonable period of time to be considered part of the bargain.

Appropriate menu descriptions are a common problem for those in the food and beverage industry. For instance, if a vegetarian customer orders lentil soup from the "vegan" section of your menu and the soup was actually made with chicken broth, the customer will have a claim against your restaurant for breach of express warranty. An additional problem presents itself if your restaurant sells canned or prepackaged signature dishes, sauces, or the like, whether through a website, catalog, or ad. Any statements made in catalogs, ads, or your website will likely be considered part of the basis of the bargain for those making purchases.

Samples and Models

An express warranty can also be created by the use of samples or models, such as displays of synthetic representations of your dishes. There's a distinction between a sample and a model. A sample is drawn from the actual goods that are the subject of the sale, so the sample is presumed to embody the qualities of the goods being offered unless the seller specifically states otherwise. For instance, if you provide a customer a sip of your flagship IPA from the tap, an express warranty will be created that the growler of that IPA you sell the customer will taste the same.

A model doesn't have to be drawn from the exact group of goods that are the subject of the sale. This might apply when your restaurant buys flatware based on a heavyweight model provided by a salesperson. If the actual flatware delivered is only medium weight, then the vendor might have breached the express warranty of quality.

In Plain English

While the UCC doesn't expressly deal with services, courts typically apply the same rules to services.

IMPLIED WARRANTIES

In addition to express warranties, the UCC creates a number of implied warranties that are presumed to be part of the sales transaction.

Merchantability

The implied warranty of merchantability applies when the seller is a merchant. Merchants are defined as people who deal with goods of the kind involved in the sale or who, by their occupation, hold themselves out as having particular knowledge or skill. Merchants can also be people this knowledge or skill is attributed to because they're acting as agents for a merchant. What is merchantability? Consider:

- Does the item pass without objection in the trade under the description given in the contract between the buyer and seller?

- Is the item fit for the ordinary purposes such goods are used for?
- Is the item adequately contained, packaged, and labeled as required by the contract or usage of trade?
- Does the item run within the variation range permitted by the contract?
- Are the items of a consistent kind, quality, and quantity within each unit and among units?
- Does the item conform to any promises made on its container or label?

An item need not be perfect to be merchantable. Trade usage (the norms of a particular trade) also establishes the particular qualities that are acceptable for items produced by members of that trade. Generally, the higher an item is priced, the more justifiable is the buyer's expectation of high quality.

Where the product is food, it must be "wholesome" to be considered merchantable. Wholesome food is free from foreign materials and dangerous substances (including bacteria that cause food poisoning). In determining whether food is wholesome, reasonable expectations may be considered. For example, a chicken bone in a chicken potpie, a fish bone in a fish chowder, and a walnut shell in walnut ice cream are often seen as risks that should have been expected and guarded against by the consumer. Some courts have held that a "natural" harmful substance like those discussed above is never a breach of the implied warranty of merchantability. Items such as glass or rocks are different since a consumer wouldn't have any reason to suspect those hazards.

Particular Purpose

When a seller knows the buyer is purchasing the goods for a particular purpose and that the buyer is relying on the seller's skill or judgment to select something suitable, there is an implied warranty that the goods will fit that purpose. A particular purpose means a specific purpose for a specific buyer's use, not just an ordinary use. The usual way this warranty is created is when the buyer asks the seller for help choosing a product.

Imagine that a restaurant patron asks which gluten-free items on the menu are good, and the server suggests the chili. If the chili is made with bulgur, this recommendation breaches the implied warranty of fitness for a particular purpose. An exception to this warranty is when a buyer asks for a particular brand (e.g., a customer orders a glass of Screaming Eagle Cabernet Sauvignon). In that case, the buyer isn't relying on the seller's skill and judgment, so no implied warranty is created.

Title

A warranty of title is implied in every contract for the sale of goods. It simply means that the seller has good title (the right to sell the item) and is unaware of any outstanding lien against the item. The seller doesn't need to be a merchant as defined above and isn't protected from liability by ignorance of a defect in the title. If you buy a commercial rice cooker through eBay and the cooker turns out to have been stolen, the seller has breached this warranty.

Infringement

The most modern of the implied warranties is the implied warranty against infringement. When an item is sold, the seller warrants that the item doesn't infringe any patent, trademark, copyright, or trade dress rights. If the object was created in violation of a third person's intellectual property rights—say it's a bootlegged copy of Microsoft Office—this warranty is breached.

DISCLAIMERS

You might decide to use a disclaimer when you don't want to give one or more of the warranties mentioned above. To be effective, disclaimers must be given in certain specific ways and in writing, so ask your lawyer for help drafting disclaimers suitable for your particular situation.

Oral Agreements

Sometimes a customer claims that oral warranties were made before they signed a written contract. The seller might be shielded from this problem by a rule that sometimes prevents prior oral statements from being considered as part of the contract, but in many states, if the situation involves an unfair trade practice, then all prior oral statements are admissible. Further, if the oral terms are consistent with a written disclaimer, they'll be binding if the writing wasn't intended as a complete and exclusive statement of the terms.

Express Warranties

Once you've given an express warranty, it's difficult to disclaim it. After all, it seems unreasonable to give an express warranty and then turn around and take it away. This means that any attempt to disclaim an express warranty will usually be unsuccessful.

Implied Warranties

In most states, implied warranties can be disclaimed. To exclude or modify the implied warranty of merchantability, the word *merchantability* must be specifically mentioned, and the disclaimer must be conspicuous. This warranty can be disclaimed orally, but it could be hard to prove that you'd done so. The implied warranty of fitness for a particular purpose can be disclaimed only in writing, and the implied warranty of title can be disclaimed only by specific language or by circumstances that give the buyer reason to know that the seller either doesn't have title or that the seller's title is subject to a third party's interest.

In Plain English

Consult with an attorney regarding the warranties you want to disclaim and the best method of accomplishing your goal. The rules on disclaimers are quite technical, and unfair trade practice laws may override any disclaimers.

MAGNUSON-MOSS WARRANTY ACT

If you decide to give a written warranty or disclaim warranty protection in writing, you should be aware that federal regulations promulgated under the Magnuson-Moss Warranty Act cover consumer products. This act includes a long list of things that must be spelled out in a written warranty, including:

- who the warranty is for (just the buyer? or future owners as well?);
- exactly which parts of the product are covered;
- what the warrantor will do in case of a defect or malfunction;
- when the warranty begins and ends;
- what the buyer has to do to get warranty coverage, including any money that must be paid;

- the names and addresses of the warrantors;
- any limitations on the duration of implied warranties (this isn't allowed in some states);
- any exclusions or limitations.

In the written warranty, you must also specify what you're promising regarding the material and workmanship, specify that the item is defect-free or meets a specific level of performance, and clearly indicate whether the warranty is full or limited.

Under a full warranty, warranty service is free of charge, there's no limitation on the duration of implied warranties, and the seller will remedy the problem with the product within a reasonable period of time. The seller must replace the item or refund the purchase price if the item is unsuccessfully repaired numerous times. Consequential damages aren't excluded or limited unless this is clear on the face of the warranty, and warranty service is for any owner of the item, not just the original buyer. If any one of these qualifications isn't met, you've given (or received) a limited warranty, not a full warranty.

REMEDIES

If you breach a warranty and the buyer is damaged by your failure to comply with your warranty obligations, a court might order you to pay damages, court costs, and in some instances reasonable attorney's fees. Since this remedy exists, you should be careful to determine which warranties you're giving and learn how to disclaim them if you don't want to give them. Similarly, you should carefully review the warranties of all items you plan to purchase—you may discover that another vendor offers a better warranty.

USING AN ATTORNEY

Consult with a business lawyer to evaluate the extent of your exposure and whether warranty disclaimers and limitations of liability can be used in your state and specific situation. In addition, you can obtain product liability insurance (see Chapter 16, Product Liability, and Chapter 17, Business Insurance) to insulate yourself from extensive liability.

ONLINE SALES

Before selling in other countries, determine your business's potential exposure. Many countries have more restrictive laws than the United States does, so consult with an experienced business lawyer when setting up your website and commencing online sales activity unless your sales platform is set up to ship only to US addresses. Merely relying on representations from third-party vendors that they comply with all necessary laws puts your business at risk if in fact those representations are not accurate.

CHAPTER 16

Product Liability

Caveat emptor—let the buyer beware. This maxim has been repeated time and again in court decisions until relatively recent times, but the pendulum has now swung the other way and the rule has become *caveat vendor*—let the seller beware.

DEFECTIVE PRODUCTS

In nearly every state in the United States, those in the food and beverage industry are strictly liable for any personal injuries caused by the food and beverages they sell if they're defective and unreasonably dangerous. Strict liability means you can be liable for a customer's injury despite having done nothing wrong. For instance, even if your restaurant takes reasonable steps to keep its food products safe, you might have unknowingly purchased romaine lettuce contaminated with *E. coli.* If, despite your safety precautions, customers become ill, your restaurant will be liable even though it's done its best to keep its patrons safe. Your only protection against claims like this is insurance (see Chapter 17).

Other times, liability is based on the negligence of the business, that is, either doing something that a reasonably prudent person wouldn't do or failing to do something that a reasonably prudent person would do. For example, an employee of a Utah restaurant accidentally added lye to the tea dispenser instead of sugar, causing deep, ulcerated burns in the customer's upper esophagus and mouth.

Types of Product Defects

There are three kinds of product defects—manufacturing defects, design defects, and failure to warn.

1. Manufacturing Defects

A manufacturing defect occurs when there's an error in making the product. Your food and beverage business may have a product liability claim arising out of its use of equipment, such as when an industrial oven at your bakery explodes due to a malfunctioning safety valve, causing the oven door to blow off and strike an employee, or when kitchen staff are sickened by carbon monoxide poisoning because of a defective exhaust system.

You could also be liable for providing defective food or beverages. In 2015, seventy-five people died after drinking contaminated beer at a funeral in Mozambique. It was later discovered that the beer had been contaminated with the bacterium *Burkholderia gladioli*, which produces the toxic compound bongkrekic acid and toxoflavin. The investigation ultimately concluded that the brewer had used flood-damaged corn flour to make this batch of beer. Other types of food poisoning, including *E. coli* and salmonella, can arise from "manufacturing" defects. Most product-liability claims against food-service businesses like restaurants and caterers are for manufacturing defects.

Manufacturing defects also occur in product packaging. A defect may cause a glass jar to shatter when a person tries to reseal it, as happened with a jar of peanuts, resulting in the person's hand being severely cut. This is obviously of more concern to those who sell prepackaged food and beverages.

In Plain English

Keep good records of your purchases in case you need to identify the seller when a problem occurs. If, for example, a customer is injured by a bit of broken glass contained in a ketchup bottle, you might be able to pass the liability on to the ketchup maker.

2. Design Defects

Design defects are flaws in a product's design that make it unreasonably dangerous to consumers. For instance, beer cans might explode due to refermentation caused by adding fruit late in the brewing process without stabilizing the beer through the use of chemicals or pasteurization. That is, the recipe for the beer, not a mistake in making the beer, causes the problem. Similarly, a salad recipe might call for *Amanita phalloides* mushrooms, said to be the most delicious of mushrooms, but fatal in even small amounts. Your business might have a claim against the manufacturer of a fryer made with a highly flammable electrical cord, or the maker of a meat grinder without appropriate blade guards.

A design may be considered defective if it doesn't meet the standards set forth in a statute. No product should be sold for consumer use before checking to see if it's covered by a consumer protection law. This is particularly important in the case of food and beverages, which are heavily regulated by state and federal laws, including the Food, Drug, and Cosmetic Act (FDCA). A violation of these laws may carry criminal sanctions. A design can also be defective even if there are no specific laws that apply to it.

3. Marketing Defects (Failure to Warn)

A product can be defective if the user isn't appropriately warned of a danger in the product, though there's no obligation to warn of dangers that a reasonable consumer should know about, such as the fact that knives are sharp. One of the most notorious "failure to warn" cases is McDonald's failure to warn customers that it served coffee thirty to forty degrees hotter than coffee is usually served, even though it knew that many of its customers had been badly burned. Other examples of the necessity to warn include a restaurant's duty to notify patrons of the dangers of eating meals that include raw or undercooked eggs, seafood, and beef, and a blender manufacturer's failure to warn that injury may occur if the blender is operated without its lid.

PRODUCT LIABILITY CLAIMS

In every product liability case, the plaintiff must prove that:

- injury occurred to the plaintiff;
- the injury was caused by some defect in the product; and
- the defect was present in the product when the defendant had control over it.

Once people are in possession of your product, you won't be able to stop them from injuring themselves, but you can do your best to ensure that any item that leaves your control contains no defects. If, for instance, your restaurant allows takeout or if your signature dishes are packaged for sale, be sure the food is safe to eat at the time it leaves your control. If someone buying takeout, for example, gets busy at work and eats it only after it's been sitting out for several hours, your restaurant shouldn't be liable. It's a good idea to include instructions for refrigerating and heating the purchased food.

If you do have to pay damages to a customer injured through no fault of your own, such as when you've followed all safety precautions but customers are sickened by contaminated lettuce, you might be able to seek reimbursement from your supplier. Unfortunately, this may involve another expensive lawsuit, and if your supplier is broke, you're out of luck. There are two things you might do for protection: incorporate or use another business form that offers limited liability (see Chapter 1) and obtain insurance (see Chapter 17).

THINK BEFORE YOU POUR

Restaurants, brewpubs, wine-tasting rooms, caterers, and others that serve alcoholic beverages should be aware of the extent of their legal responsibility for intoxicated patrons. The amount of potential liability is staggering, often well over a million dollars and sometimes into the tens of millions. Most states have statutes imposing liability called "dram shop" or "civil damages" acts. Other states impose liability through the common law. In most states, liquor license holders are responsible for damages if they serve people who are under the legal drinking age or who are obviously intoxicated and they harm themselves, other people, or property. Owners and managers may even be personally liable for their employees' failure to follow alcoholic-beverage regulations and dram shop laws.

Arrangements should be made for individuals who have had too much to drink to be driven home, either by other guests or by taxi. Some tow companies and mass transit operators offer free or low-cost transportation services during holidays to help prevent drunk driving.

To reduce the risk of liability, servers should ask for identification from anyone who appears to be under the age of thirty before serving an alcoholic beverage and learn how to identify fake IDs. It's not always obvious when a guest is intoxicated, but servers should refuse to serve anyone who appears to have had too much to drink. Some things to look out for are slurred speech, glassy eyes, stumbling, spilling drinks, and aggressive behavior. Training of your servers should be ongoing and well documented. Follow all legal requirements in your jurisdiction, such as obtaining a liquor license, complying with its terms, and having your staff obtain required certifications.

Insurance is available for businesses that serve alcoholic beverages. In many states, having liquor liability insurance is a condition of a liquor license, and some commercial landlords require tenants that serve alcohol to have this type of insurance. Contact your insurance broker for more information about liquor liability insurance.

CHAPTER 17

Business Insurance

The forces of nature—such as fires, floods, and earthquakes—are undiscriminating in their targets, and even if your business is in a low-crime area, you might become the victim of burglary or vandalism. As discussed in the preceding chapter, your food and beverage business may be subjected to liability for food poisoning or for an accident caused by a customer served alcohol. Loss of earnings through sickness or accident is a risk common to all small businesses. These risks and others are far too often overlooked, but these occurrences can be disastrous to a small business. Fortunately, many of these risks can be insured against.

BASICS OF INSURANCE LAW

Before we analyze the mechanics of choosing whether or not to insure a particular risk, we'll briefly outline the law of insurance.

Insurable Interest

Public policy won't allow you to insure something unless you have an "insurable interest." To have an insurable interest, you must have a property right, a contract right, or a potential liability that would result in a real loss to you if a given event occurs. This is to minimize the temptation for you to cause the loss you've bought insurance to cover.

The Contract

All insurance is based on a contract between the insurer and the insured (the person or business covered by the insurance) through which the insurer assumes a specified risk for a fee called a premium. The insurance contract must contain at least all of the following:

- a description of whatever is being insured (the subject matter);
- the nature of the risks insured against;
- the maximum possible recovery;
- the duration of the insurance; and
- the due date and amount of the premiums.

When the amount of recovery has been predetermined in the insurance contract, it's called a "valued" policy. An "unvalued" policy covers the full value of property up to a specified policy limit. The forms that a company uses to make insurance contracts are regulated by each state. Sometimes the state requires a standard form that can't be modified by the insurers. Many states require "plain language" to be used in all forms. Plain language is measured in reference to the average number of syllables per word and the average number of words per sentence.

Even with these laws, policies can be difficult to understand, and after a catastrophic loss, insureds often learn that their insurers have different ideas about what their policies cover. As of this writing, for instance, restaurants and bars all over the country (including Chez Panisse and Cheers) are engaged in disputes with their insurance companies about whether their business-interruption policies cover their losses arising from closures related to COVID-19. While some policies have exclusions for pandemics, coverage is being denied for policies without those exclusions as well. At least one court has held that capacity limits can be a "direct physical loss" covered by insurance because such limitations prevent the business from using its physical space. We recommend you review your insurance policies with your attorney or with your insurance broker or agent.

In Plain English

An "agent" is a person who is employed by a single insurance company for the purpose of selling its insurance. A "broker" is a person or entity who represents a number of insurance companies and is authorized by those companies to sell its policies. Brokers customarily shop the risk to a number of companies in order to obtain the best price for the policy.

ASCERTAINING RISK

An insurance contract does more than merely shift the risk from the insured to the insurance company. The insurance industry is regulated by state law so as to spread the risk among those subject to that same risk. The risk-spreading is accomplished by defining the method used for determining the amount of the premium to be paid by the insured.

First, the insurance company obtains data on the actual losses sustained by a defined class within a given period of time. There are legal restrictions on how the insurer defines the class. An insurance company can't, for example, separate restaurants owned by white and nonwhite people into different classes, but it can separate pizza delivery chains whose drivers have many accidents from those whose drivers have few. Next, the company divides the risk equally among the members of the class and adds a fee for administrative costs and profits (usually regulated by state law). Finally, the premium is set for each individual or business in proportion to the likelihood that a loss will occur.

ADDITIONAL STATE REGULATIONS

Besides the method of determining premiums, state insurance laws usually specify the training necessary for agents and brokers, the amount of commission payable to them, and the kind of investments the insurance company may make with the premiums.

EXPECTATIONS V. REALITY

A frequent result of the complex terms used even in "plain language" insurance contracts is that the signed contract differs in some respect from what the agent may have led the insured person to expect. If you can prove that an agent actually lied, then the agent will be personally liable to you for the amount of promised coverage. In addition, the insurance company itself might be liable for the wrongful acts of its agents.

Most often, though, the agent hasn't lied, but has accidentally neglected to inform the insured of some detail. For instance, if your catering business wants insurance for transporting food, beverages, dishes, cutlery and the like, the agent may sell you a policy that covers transport only in public carriers, although you transport the products yourself. If you neglect to read the clause that limits coverage to a public carrier, you'd be out of luck in most states, because most commonly, courts hold that it's the insured's duty to read the policy before buying the insurance.

In some states this doctrine has been considered too harsh, and an insured can challenge specific provisions in the signed contract to the extent they don't conform to reasonable expectations resulting from promises that the agent made. In the example above, it might be considered reasonable for you to expect coverage when transporting your own goods. If the agent didn't specifically call your attention to this limitation in the contract, odds are good that you wouldn't be subject to the limitation.

Other states follow a different approach for contract interpretation and attempt to discover the intention of the parties. The first step in interpreting an insurance policy is to examine the text and context of the policy as a whole. If, after that examination, two or more conflicting interpretations remain reasonable, the ambiguity is resolved against the insurer.

In Plain English

Read the contract with your broker or agent. If you don't understand it, ask the broker or agent to list all of the important aspects before you sign it. Keep the explanatory note, letter, or email from the agent with the policy.

OVERINSURING AND UNDERINSURING

When insureds accidentally overvalue the items being insured, they'll still be covered, but the recovery will be only for the true value of the goods. Overinsurance doesn't entitle you to recover more than that, because you don't have an insurable interest in the objects beyond their actual value. Since you can, at best, break even with insurance, you may consider underinsuring your property so you can pay lower premiums. This has been tried and failed.

One insured stated the value of her unscheduled property (a collection of items not itemized in the policy) as $9,950 and obtained insurance on that amount. A fire caused at least $9,950 in damage. After an investigation, the insurance company determined that the insured owned at least $36,500 in unscheduled property and refused to pay on the grounds that the insured obtained the insurance fraudulently.

The court agreed with the insurance company, stating that the intentional failure to communicate the full value of the unscheduled property rendered the entire contract void, which meant the insured couldn't even collect the policy maximum. Although at first glance this may seem harsh, its ultimate fairness becomes apparent with a little analysis. The odds of losing $9,950 out of $36,500 is greater than the chance of losing $9,950 out of $9,950, simply because most accidents or thefts don't result in total losses.

Courts use various tests to determine whether an omission or misstatement renders a policy void. Usually, the policy won't be void unless the omission or misstatement is "material" and is either intentional or obviously reckless. Materiality is typically measured with reference to the degree of importance that the insurance company assigns to the omitted or misstated fact. If the insured's representations were accurate, would the insurance company have required different conditions or premiums? If so, the fact is likely material. In the above example, if the insured had disclosed the full value of the unscheduled property, the insurer would have either demanded that the full value be insured or charged a higher premium, so the misstatement was material.

UNINTENTIONAL UNDERVALUING

Not all undervaluations are material, and many insurance contracts allow for some unintentional undervaluation to protect the insured from inflation. A "coinsurance clause" generally provides that the insured can recover 100 percent of any loss up to the face value of the policy so long as the property is insured for at least 80 percent of its full value. For instance, if distillery equipment worth $100,000 were insured for $80,000 and suffered a $79,000 loss from a covered casualty, the insured would recover the full amount of the loss, or $79,000. If, however, the property was insured for $50,000, the insurer would determine the ratio of the insurance coverage to the total value of the property and multiply the resulting fraction by the loss to get the recovery.

In Plain English

Always carry insurance on at least 80 percent of the value of your property. Considering inflation, it's wise to reexamine your coverage each year. Some policies automatically increase the coverage annually, based on a fixed percentage.

PROPERTY COVERED

All insurance policies are limited to specifically described subject matter and to losses caused to that subject matter by certain defined risks. Correctly defining the subject matter of insurance is tricky business. Mistakes here are not uncommon and can result in you finding yourself uninsured.

Scheduling Property

A typical insurance policy includes various exclusions and exemptions. For example, most homeowner and auto insurance policies cover personal property, but exclude business property. After a loss, the insurance company might deny coverage for personal items related to your business that you keep at home. To avoid the potentially uninsured loss of that property, you can "schedule" the items by submitting a list and description of all pieces to be insured with an appraisal of their value. The insurer assumes the risk of loss of all scheduled items whether or not they pertain to your business. Insurance on scheduled property is usually slightly more expensive than that on unscheduled property.

Valuing Scheduled Property

Many battles occur over the value of objects stolen, destroyed, or lost. In anticipation of such battles, you should maintain records of sales and purchases. In the case of certain kinds of property (original artwork decorating your restaurant, for instance), the value must be determined by an expert in the field, although this won't prevent all problems, because the insurance company can always contest the scheduled value.

WHEN AND HOW TO INSURE

Three factors should be weighed to determine whether or not to obtain insurance. First, what's the value of the thing you're considering insuring? Health is of the utmost value, so health insurance should be a priority. Material goods are valued according to the cost of replacement. If you keep a large inventory of ingredients or if you own expensive bakery equipment, it should probably be insured. You may also want to consider obtaining business-interruption insurance. The easiest way to decide whether the value is high enough that you need to insure is to ask yourself how much it would hurt to lose it.

Second, you must estimate the chances (risk) that a certain calamity will occur. An insurance broker can tell you what risks are prevalent in your industry and in your neighborhood. Supplement this information with your personal knowledge. Although these facts should be weighed in your decision, don't tempt fate. In most situations, if the odds are truly slim, but some risk is still present, the premium will be correspondingly small. The third factor is the cost of the insurance.

Some types of insurance are required by law. For example, workers' compensation insurance is customarily required for every business with employees, though some states have exceptions for the owner of a business or members of its board of directors. Consult with your business lawyer or insurance professional regarding the laws in your state to see which types of insurance are required.

Other types of insurance aren't required by law but are, practically speaking, necessary. If your business owns its building, obtain insurance for that building. Even if your business rents, you'll need to insure the contents of the building. As we discussed in Chapter 16, you should consider obtaining product liability insurance as well. Most businesses purchase "general business liability" policies to cover a host of business risks. It's essential for you to work with an experienced business lawyer to determine the kind of insurance that will best serve your business needs.

In Plain English

Bear in mind that insurance purchased to cover your business is tax deductible. This means that if you pay tax at the rate of 21 percent, Uncle Sam is theoretically paying for 21 percent of your premium.

KEEPING THE COST DOWN

As we mentioned earlier, the premiums charged by an insurance company are regulated by state governments. Nonetheless, it still pays to shop around, especially in states with less regulation. Even in states with tight control over premiums, insurance companies can compete by offering different packages of insurance and by hiring competent agents to assist you in your choice.

If there are enough small-business owners in your area engaged in a similar business of similar size, you might form a co-op insurance fund. To do this, estimate the total losses your co-op will sustain in the course of a year. Each member contributes a pro rata share of that amount, and the money is put into a bank account. If a disaster occurs and the losses are greater than the fund, each member contributes to make up the difference. If there's any money left over, it can be used to lessen the following year's premiums. This method is cheaper than conventional insurance because it eliminates insurance agents' commissions and the insurance company's profit. Contact an attorney to determine what regulations exist in your state and for help memorializing the arrangement with a clear written agreement.

CHAPTER 18

People Who Work for You

There comes a time in the life of almost every small business when it's necessary to get help, be it brain or brawn. The help most commonly needed first for a very small business, such as an owner-operated coffee cart or a home-based baker who sells pastries to coffee shops, is a bookkeeper or accountant who can handle taxes, accounts payable, and billing. When things get a little hectic, or you just need a vacation, you might hire a barista or an assistant baker.

For a business like a restaurant or brewpub, you'll almost certainly need employees from the beginning. This chapter offers only a brief guide to basic employment issues. For more information, see another book in this series, *Employment Law (in Plain English)*®, by Leonard D. DuBoff, Kenneth Perea, Christopher Perea, and Lauren Barnes.

CLASSIFICATION OF WORKERS

Businesses often prefer to characterize their workers as independent contractors instead of employees since independent contractors are responsible for their own taxes, including FICA taxes (Medicare and Social Security), and aren't subject to many of the laws protecting employees, like wage-and-hour laws. If, however, you treat someone as an independent contractor and that person is recharacterized as an employee by a government agency, significant penalties may be imposed. Also, workers who believe they've been misclassified as independent contractors are increasingly filing lawsuits against their employers.

Several factors are considered when determining whether a worker is an employee or an independent contractor. No one factor is determinative, and these factors vary from state to state. The factors also differ depending on the purpose for which the worker is characterized—in the same state, the test is likely to be different when characterizing workers for tax purposes rather than for workers' compensation purposes.

Generally speaking, though, when people are under the direction and control of the employer, it's more likely they'll be characterized as employees. If workers perform similar tasks for several different employers and function independently, it's more probable that they'll be characterized as independent contractors. When employers provide the tools, equipment, and a place to work, it's more likely that the workers will be characterized as employees, but if they provide their own equipment and supplies, the argument that the workers are independent contractors is strengthened. The place where the work is performed, whether the workers have their own business licenses, as well as other relevant factors, may also be considered when determining workers' status.

To strengthen the argument that a worker is independent, have a written contract requiring the worker to furnish all tools, materials, and equipment necessary to perform the work; to obtain all required business registrations, permits, and licenses; and to be responsible for hiring, paying, supervising, and firing any employees working for that person. When assigning the work, allow the worker as much flexibility as possible with respect to how the work will be done—your company's main concern should be the finished product. A contract saying the worker is an independent contractor is never enough to characterize a worker as an independent contractor—the way the worker is supervised and how the work is actually done must also meet the independent-contractor test.

In Plain English

You might think misclassifying employees as independent contractors will save you money, but it's likely to cost you a lot more, since in addition to owing back taxes, you may be fined by multiple government agencies and sued by misclassified workers for unpaid overtime, vacation pay, and compensation for other benefits.

INDEPENDENT CONTRACTORS

Although you're paying these workers for their services, independent contractors remain their own bosses and can even hire others to do the work on their behalf. Many employers feel that's a reasonable trade-off for the benefits, though. These include not having to pay FICA taxes, withhold income taxes, obtain a workers' compensation policy, or comply with the myriad other rules imposed on employers.

Liability

Although employers don't often recognize this benefit of hiring independent contractors, you're usually not liable for injuries to a third party resulting from an independent contractor's negligence or wrongful acts while working for you. There are, however, situations when independent contractors can render you legally responsible for their wrongful acts. These situations fall into the following three basic categories.

1. If an employer is careless in hiring or retaining an independent contractor and a careful investigation would have disclosed facts indicating that the independent contractor wasn't qualified, the employer will be liable when the independent contractor fails to properly perform the job and a third person is injured. For instance, you might hire an independent contractor to install ceiling fans in your bar without first checking with your state's construction contractors' board to verify that this person has the appropriate licenses. If the fans aren't installed properly and one falls, both you and the independent contractor will be liable to any injured patrons.
2. If a job is so dangerous as to be characterized as ultrahazardous or inherently dangerous (both legal terms) and is to be performed for the employer's benefit, then regardless of who performs the work, the employer is legally responsible for any injuries that occur during the performance of the work. If, for example, you hire an independent contractor to walk trained tigers through your restaurant to visit with patrons, you (along with the tiger trainer) will be liable for any injuries the tigers cause.

3. An employer may be required by law to perform certain tasks for the health and safety of the community. Imagine that you hire an independent contractor to clear ice from the sidewalk in front of your restaurant, a spot is missed, and someone slips and is injured. In this situation, both you and the independent contractor will be liable.

These responsibilities are said to be nondelegable. If a nondelegable duty is performed by an independent contractor, the employer is responsible for any injury that results.

EMPLOYEES

Employees are typically anyone over whose work you exercise direct control—examples are managers, hosts, waitstaff, cooks, chefs, dishwashers, bartenders, bussers, delivery drivers, brewers, vintners, wine-club managers, special-event coordinators, and salespeople who represent only your business. The formation of this relationship entails nothing more than an agreement on your side to hire someone and an agreement by that person to work. Although a written contract usually isn't necessary, you should put employment terms down in writing, especially for upper-level employees, so that there are no misunderstandings later. In addition, every business ought to have an employee handbook describing its policies and procedures.

Liability

You're always liable for the negligence and—sometimes, even the intentional wrongdoing—of your employees when they're acting on your behalf. For instance, if your employee is at fault in an automobile accident while driving your ice cream truck, you'll be liable regardless of how carefully you've screened your drivers. This means you should be extremely careful when hiring and make sure you have appropriate insurance coverage.

Employment Details

1. Term, Termination, and Discipline

Employment can be either terminable at will or for a fixed duration. If a fixed-duration term of employment is to be for more than one year, you must have a written contract specifying the period of employment; otherwise, either party can terminate the relationship at any time. A fixed term has some advantages. It gives the employee job security and creates an obligation for the employee to remain for the full term, which is good for your business, but it also means neither of you can terminate the arrangement except for the reasons spelled out in the contract. Of course, if the employee wants to quit or you want to fire the employee, the law won't require you and the employee to work together for the remainder of the term. Improper premature termination does, however, subject the terminating party to liability for damages.

At-will employment means that both the employee and the employer can terminate employment for any reason— or even no reason at all, though employers are prohibited by state and federal laws from terminating employment for reasons such as race-based discrimination. In most states (as of this writing, Montana is the only exception), employment is presumed to be at will unless a labor union is involved. In Montana, after a probationary period, employers can terminate their employees' employment only for good cause. An at-will arrangement has its own advantages since the employee and employer work together only so long as they both want to. Employers can terminate underperforming employees, and employees are free to quit to pursue better opportunities elsewhere.

Spell out the grounds for discipline and termination of employment, even when employment is terminable at will, in which case you should clearly specify that you can terminate the employment either for the specified causes or at will and that you aren't required to follow a set disciplinary procedure. We recommend you include a statement similar to this in your employee handbook: "We have sole discretion to determine under what circumstances discipline and discharge are appropriate. We reserve the right to terminate employment at any time for any reason or no reason at all, as well as to skip progressive discipline."

In progressive discipline, an employer starts by orally warning an employee of a problem and progressively imposing disciplinary practices until termination becomes the only form of recourse left. Obviously, this isn't a good approach for major problems like violence or theft, but it can be used to give an employee an opportunity to correct problems with performance or tardiness.

Language in employee handbooks and oral statements made by recruiters or interviewers are sometimes construed as giving rise to a contractual right to employment. To avoid this problem, put a legend in your employee handbook making it clear that the handbook isn't an employment contract ("Nothing in this Handbook or in any document or statement and nothing implied from any course of conduct will limit our or your right to terminate employment at will").

It's also wise to require prospective employees to sign a statement making it clear that their employment is at will—this is often combined with an acknowledgment of receipt of the employee handbook. Further, if you have an "introductory" or "probationary" period for new employees, say that at the end of that period, the probationary employee will become a "regular" or "full-time" employee—not a "permanent" one.

2. Wages and Tips

If you have gross sales of $500,000 or more or are engaged in interstate commerce (which is broadly defined), you'll have to comply with federal minimum-wage and overtime laws. Most states have their own minimum-wage and overtime laws that must be followed as well. Above the requirements imposed by these laws, the amount of compensation is open to bargaining.

If no wage is specified, the law presumes a reasonable wage for the work performed, so you can't escape paying your employees fairly by not discussing the amount they'll earn. Some state and local laws regulate sick time, holidays, and vacations, as well as the method and timing of paying employees during employment and upon termination. This area of the law changes rapidly, and employees may even have additional rights temporarily, like the new or increased paid sick leave required during the COVID-19 pandemic. On top of an hourly wage or salary, other benefits can be given, such as health and life insurance or retirement pensions. Some legal advice in this area can help you take full advantage of the tax laws.

Tips are common in the food and beverage industry, and in some states, this might affect how much you have to pay your tipped employees. The federal minimum wage law and some state counterparts have special rules for tipped employees. The Fair Labor Standards Act (FLSA) defines a "tipped employee" as one who regularly receives more than thirty dollars per month in tips. Under federal law, you can consider these tips as part of your waitstaff's wages, but you also have to pay them a minimum of $2.13 per hour in direct wages. Check the laws of your state, though, since many states don't allow tip credits.

If you can use tip credits and choose to do so, you must tell the involved employees about the cash wage and the claimed tip credit in advance. You also have to let them know that the tip credit can't exceed the amount of tips actually received and that all tips are kept by the tipped employee (except in the case of a valid tip-pooling arrangement). Finally, you must be able to prove that tipped employees receive at least the minimum wage when their regular wages and the tip credit allowance are combined.

In 2018, the Department of Labor (DOL) relaxed its rules about tip credits when employees perform some duties that are tipped and some that aren't. Now, according to DOL guidance, an employer can apply the tip credit to all hours worked by an employee in a tipped occupation, as long as the non-tipped duties are "related to" the tipped occupation and performed either at the same time as the tipped duties or during a "reasonable" time immediately before or after the tipped duties. Examples are setting and bussing tables. A final rule announced by the DOL in December 2020 codifies this guidance, but as of this writing, the DOL has delayed the effective date of three portions of the rule, including those related to tipped and nontipped duties. Unless this part of the rule becomes effective, the tip credit can't be used if nontipped duties exceeded 20 percent of the time worked.

A now-effective part of the new rule prohibits any arrangement between an employer and a tipped employee by which any part of the tip received becomes the employer's property. A tip personally given to an employee by a patron belongs to that employee unless the business has a tip-pooling arrangement limited to employees who customarily and regularly receive tips. The new final rule also allows employers that don't take the tip credit to implement mandatory tip pools that include employees who do not customarily receive tips—but not managers or supervisors.

The FLSA doesn't impose a maximum contribution amount or percentage on mandatory tip pools, but it does require employers to notify tipped employees of any required tip-pool contribution amount. The employer can take a tip credit only for the amount each tipped employee ultimately receives and can't retain any of the employees' tips for any other purpose.

Have employees who participate in tip-pooling arrangements sign a tip-pooling consent form so you can prove that you gave them the appropriate notices. Except as noted previously, by law, tipped employees can't be required to share their tips with restaurant personnel who don't customarily receive tips (like dishwashers and cooks), but you can deduct the fees levied by the credit card company for charged tips.

Another now-effective part of the new final rule explicitly prohibits employers (including managers and supervisors) from keeping employees' tips for any purpose—whether not the employer takes a tip credit, requires employers that collect tips to facilitate mandatory tip pools to fully redistribute the tips no less often than when they pay wages, and incorporates a new recordkeeping requirement for employers that do not take a tip credit but collect employees' tips to operate a mandatory tip pool.

An Advice Memorandum issued in October 2020 by the National Labor Relations Board (NLRB) found that employees who discussed and complained about their employer's tip-pooling practices engaged in protected concerted activity and that when a steakhouse fired the employees for their complaints and discussions, it violated the National Labor Relations Act. Even nonunionized workers have the right to engage in "concerted activities for the purpose of collective bargaining or other mutual aid or protection," and the NLRB has held that certain types of conversations, such as those about work conditions, are considered "inherently concerted," even when the employees aren't unionized and aren't thinking of taking any group action.

3. Time Worked

In some situations, you must pay employees for preparatory and concluding activities that aren't part of their work assignment. One example is an employee putting on and taking off a uniform. An employer has to pay for this time only if it requires employees to do so on the employer's premises. You don't have to pay them if they have the option of changing at home.

4. Duties

It's wise to spell out your employee's duties in a written job description or employment contract. This serves as a form of orientation for the employee and may reduce future conflicts over what the job entails. In addition, it's helpful to have a detailed job description when you conduct reviews and when you're determining whether an applicant can handle the job.

5. Predictive Scheduling

Predictive-scheduling laws require employers to post employees' work schedules a certain number of days in advance (usually seven to fourteen days). Oregon is, as of the time of this writing, the only state with such a law, but many cities—including San Francisco, Chicago, New York, Philadelphia, and Seattle—require predictive scheduling.

6. Noncompetition, Nonsolicitation, and Proprietary Information

You might want your employees to agree not to compete against you after the end of their employment, either on their own or as employees of competing businesses. This type of agreement is unenforceable in some states; in others, it must be carefully written to comply with the relevant state law. In some states, an agreement not to solicit your customers after termination of employment is enforceable even if noncompetition provisions are prohibited. Because this is a complex area of the law, consult with an experienced business lawyer when preparing any noncompetition or nonsolicitation agreement.

Provisions restricting the use of your business's intellectual property, including trade secrets, are enforceable in every state. These restrictions should always be in writing. Trade secrets may include, among other things, customer lists, supplier lists, secret formulas, and know-how. For more information, see Chapter 9, Patents and Trade Secrets.

7. Other Considerations in Hiring

There are many other issues you need to consider when hiring an employee. These include, but aren't limited to:

- A workers' compensation policy for your employees in the event of on-the-job injury or occupational illness. State laws vary on the minimum number of employees that trigger this requirement. In many states, an employer who fails to obtain or keep in force required workers' compensation insurance is liable for any on-the-job injury or illness, whether or not the employer is at fault. This includes not only medical expenses, but also damages for pain and suffering, lost earning potential, and other damages arising from on-the-job injuries or illnesses.
- Withholding federal, state, and local taxes, including FICA. The laws vary in different states and municipalities, so you'll need to find out what's required in your area. Failure to withhold taxes as required by law exposes the employer to liability for that amount plus interest and penalties.

- Unemployment insurance, which is a joint state-federal program.
- Health and safety regulations (both federal and state), including those that may be put in place temporarily, such as governors' orders issued during the COVID-19 pandemic.
- Employee benefits like insurance coverage (medical, dental, prepaid legal), retirement benefits, memberships, and parking.
- Union requirements, if you or your employees are subject to union contracts.
- Limitations on drug testing, background checks, and using information related to prior convictions (a.k.a. "ban the box" laws).
- Special rules relating to the employment of minors.
- Verification of work eligibility (the Department of Justice often targets businesses in the food and beverage industry for investigation).

Because these laws vary from place to place, you should discuss them with your lawyer and accountant. Also find out if any other forms of employment legislation, like licensing or certification requirements, apply to your employees. Common requirements for workers in the food and beverage industry include food handlers' permits and alcohol service permits.

Hazards in the Workplace

While few small-business owners would intentionally injure a fellow human being, your business is likely to require employees to engage in some hazardous activities. Businesses in the food and beverage industry often use toxic materials, especially for cleaning, but sometimes for cooking (as in the use of lye for pretzels). Occupational Safety and Health Administration (OSHA) regulations require that all employers with hazardous chemicals in their workplaces provide labels and Material Safety Data Sheets (MSDS) for their exposed workers and train them to handle the chemicals appropriately. More information on this can be found at the OSHA website at www.osha.gov.

Your state workers' compensation agency and state OSHA might also have safety rules applicable to your business—obtain a lawyer's assistance to determine whether any of these regulations apply to your particular business.

A paragraph containing the required disclosures about hazardous substances and the employee's acknowledgment of the known risks should be incorporated into your employee handbook and any employment contracts. While these documents won't provide a defense to a workers' compensation claim, they'll make employees aware of the need for caution in working with the hazardous materials.

Of course, hazardous chemicals aren't the only concern. Businesses in the food and beverage industry usually have a lot of tools and equipment that can result in cuts and burns, like knives, grinders, slicers, ovens, grills, and fryers. Tripping over extension cords, slipping on greasy or wet floors, and climbing fermentation-tank ladders may result in falls, and carrying heavy trays, bags, or boxes can cause injuries, as may frequently moving in a repetitive way. Some businesses are prone to robberies. Finally, as the COVID-19 outbreak made clear, employees must be protected from contagious illnesses, for their own health as well as that of your customers.

Needless to say, you should take all precautions possible to protect the health and safety of your employees, both because it's the right thing to do and because you may be subjected to financial penalties if you fail to comply with safety regulations.

Discrimination

Business owners must comply with numerous antidiscrimination laws, including the Civil Rights Act, the Equal Pay Act, the Age Discrimination in Employment Act, and the Americans with Disabilities Act. The Equal Employment Opportunity Commission (EEOC) and similar state agencies are responsible for enforcement of these laws. These laws generally prohibit not only intentional discrimination but practices that have the effect of discrimination. They apply to all aspects of hiring, transfer, promotion, layoff, and termination, including job advertisements, recruitment, testing, use of company facilities, training, benefits, leave, and discipline. Many antidiscrimination laws apply to independent contractors as well as to employees.

These laws also prohibit management from retaliating against employees or job applicants who file discrimination charges against them. A business found to have unlawfully discriminated will likely be liable for lost wages, as well as punitive and other damages, including attorneys' fees. In this section, we discuss only federal laws, but many states, as well as some counties and cities, have their own antidiscrimination laws, and these are often more protective of employees than the federal law, so be sure to ask your attorney for information regarding the antidiscrimination laws that apply to your business.

1. Civil Rights Act

The Civil Rights Act prohibits discrimination based on race, color, religion, national origin, or sex. Race-based discrimination includes discrimination based on skin color, hair texture, and facial features, as well as harassment and segregation. It also includes discrimination based on a person's marriage to or association with those of a different race.

With limited exceptions for faith-based employment, employers are prohibited from treating employees or applicants less or more favorably because of their religious beliefs or practices. Employers can't force employees to participate or refrain from participating in a religious activity as a condition of employment. Employers must reasonably accommodate employees' sincerely held religious beliefs and permit employees to engage in religious expression if employees are permitted to engage in other personal expressions at work. This law also requires the employer to take steps to prevent religious harassment of their employees, not only by other employees and management but also by vendors and customers.

Compliance may also require scheduling accommodations. For example, a jury awarded a Catholic dishwasher $21.5 million in 2019 after finding that her employer had violated her religious rights by repeatedly scheduling her to work on Sundays and ultimately firing her.

National-origin discrimination includes discrimination based on foreign accents and English fluency, as well as English-only rules, though there are exceptions for rules that are necessary for the safe or efficient operation of the business. The prohibitions against sex-based discrimination encompass pregnancy, birth, and related medical conditions, as well as sexual harassment. The Equal Pay Act prohibits sex-based wage discrimination among persons in the same establishment who are performing under similar working conditions. More information about illegal discrimination can be obtained at the EEOC's website, www.eeoc.gov.

2. Harassment

Harassment based on protected characteristics like gender or race is a form of illegal discrimination. You should have written policies prohibiting discriminatory language (e.g., ethnic jokes or religious slurs) and other offensive language or activities, as well as a detailed sexual harassment policy. There are two basic types of sexual harassment: quid pro quo and hostile environment. Quid pro quo refers to harassers asking for sexual favors in exchange for some advantage in the workplace or harassers penalizing those who reject their sexual advances.

A hostile environment, on the other hand, is more generalized in that the harasser creates or permits a hostile work environment through language, activities, or conduct. If, for instance, a restaurant manager frequently makes racial slurs to waitstaff or repeatedly tells female cooks they'll never be promoted to sous-chef because women become hysterical under pressure, the manager will be liable.

If a supervisor has harassed or permitted harassment of an employee resulting in a tangible employment action such as demotion or termination, the employer is liable for the discriminatory actions of its supervisor, but if there's been no tangible job action, the employer is only presumed liable for the supervisor's harassment. The employer might be able to avoid liability if it can prove that it had and enforced an appropriate policy against the type of harassment at issue and that the complaining employee unreasonably failed to take advantage of any preventive or corrective opportunities offered by the employer.

In Plain English

Sexual misconduct by a key employee can be devastating to a business. After a number of women accused chef Mario Batali of sexual harassment and sexual misconduct, he was fired from ABC's *The Chew*, Target pulled his pasta sauces and cookbooks, and his company closed its three Las Vegas Strip restaurants after the Las Vegas Sands Corp. terminated the companies' relationship. In 2019, Batali surrendered ownership of his stakes in all his remaining restaurants.

3. Age Discrimination

Federal laws prohibiting age discrimination apply to those with twenty or more employees, as well as to government and union offices. These laws prohibit employers from discriminating against persons forty years old or older due to their age in connection with any term, condition, or privilege of employment. Some state laws protect younger workers as well.

4. Disabilities Discrimination

The Americans with Disabilities Act (ADA) prohibits discrimination against persons with disabilities in public accommodations, transportation, telecommunications and, most relevant for this chapter, employment. The ADA's employment-related provisions apply only to those who employ fifteen or more individuals. For purposes of the ADA, an "individual with a disability" means a person who has a physical or mental impairment that substantially limits one or more major life activities, has a record of such an impairment, or who is regarded as having such an impairment. A "qualified individual with a disability" is someone who, with or without reasonable accommodation, can perform the essential functions of the job.

Reasonable accommodation must be made so that a qualified applicant or employee with a disability can perform the necessary and essential work of the job position. Reasonable accommodations include making existing employee facilities readily accessible to and usable by disabled employees. For example, you might need to modify a person's work schedule, alter the height of a desk, install brighter lighting, or allow more frequent breaks.

A business isn't required to provide reasonable accommodations if doing so will result in an undue hardship. "Undue hardship" under the ADA refers to an action requiring significant difficulty or expense when considered in light of factors like the employer's size and financial resources. In food-based businesses, there are also special rules that apply with respect to illnesses transmissible through food.

Complex rules apply to many ADA provisions, including when and how you can require medical examinations, so contact an attorney for more information if you plan to require any physical examinations or ask health-related questions, or if you need to make accommodations for an employee with a disability. For more information concerning the Americans with Disabilities Act, see www.ada.gov.

Employee Handbooks and Training

As discussed elsewhere in this chapter, your business should have an employee handbook. Be sure to include your policies on sexual harassment and nondiscrimination and the processes for an employee to file a complaint and that complaint to be investigated. Hours of work, overtime, meal and rest breaks, dress code, and trade secret protection should be addressed, as well as any policies you have for conduct, vacation, sick time, holidays, and leave. The handbook must make it clear that it isn't an employment contract and that employment is at will.

If you plan to monitor your employees' Internet usage, emails, computer files, phone calls, voicemail messages and the like; use video surveillance; or conduct searches of employees' personal belongings, you need a specific written employee privacy policy identifying the types of situations where employees shouldn't have an expectation of privacy. Your employees do have certain privacy rights, such as privacy in the restroom, and the policy should make that clear. Also, any monitoring must be done in a nondiscriminatory manner to ensure equality, and you must equitably enforce policies and standards.

You should have a zero-tolerance policy regarding discrimination. An employee handbook containing policies against sexual harassment, offensive behaviors and the like is a good starting point. A well-drafted discrimination policy applies to behavior and to oral and written (including electronic) communications. It explains the procedures for making complaints and investigating claims. It's a good idea to provide employees with ongoing education with respect to employment relations, including harassment and discrimination issues.

In some areas, this training is required by law, so check with your attorney if you're not sure about the laws in your jurisdiction. For instance, effective in 2021, all California businesses with five or more employees must provide sexual-harassment-prevention training to all workers. Because of the #metoo and #BLM movements, these types of laws are likely to become more common. Even if it's not required for your business, regular training for all of your staff, especially supervisors, is a good idea to reduce your risk of liability.

Your employee handbook must be drafted or reviewed by a business attorney, since this area of the law changes frequently, and there are numerous requirements for legal notices and other areas that a layperson or even handbook software may fail to properly address.

The Family Medical Leave Act

The Family and Medical Leave Act of 1993 (FMLA) allows employees to take up to twelve weeks of unpaid leave each year for certain family or medical reasons if they've worked for the employer for a year and meet certain other eligibility requirements. FMLA must be followed by private-sector employers who have or have had fifty or more employees during the current or preceding calendar year and who are engaged in interstate commerce or any activity affecting commerce.

An eligible employee can take twelve weeks of leave:

- for the birth of a child and to care for the newborn child within one year of birth;
- the placement with the employee of a child for adoption or foster care and to care for the newly placed child within one year of placement;
- to care for the employee's spouse, child, or parent who has a serious health condition;
- for a serious health condition that makes the employee unable to perform the essential functions of the job; or
- for any qualifying reason arising out of the fact that the employee's spouse, son, daughter, or parent is a covered military member on "covered active duty."

Twenty-six weeks of leave are available to care for a covered servicemember with a serious injury or illness if the eligible employee is the servicemember's spouse, son, daughter, parent, or next of kin (military caregiver leave).

When the worker returns to the job, the job may be the exact job that the employee left or an equivalent job—with equivalent duties, pay, benefits and the like, though there's an exception for "key" employees whose absence from their positions will cause "substantial and grievous economic injury" to the employer. There are certain notice requirements, as well as rules about employers requiring medical certification of the need for leave. Further information can be found at www.dol.gov.

Wrongful Termination

Historically, an employee who was not under contract could be terminated for any reason whatsoever. Now in most situations, an employee's job can be terminated for the right reason or for no reason at all, but it can't be terminated for the wrong reason. For example, firing an employee for refusing to commit perjury before a legislative committee is a wrongful termination. The public policy of having individuals testify honestly is more important than the employer's right to control the employment relationship. Wrongful termination cases typically fall into certain categories. Employers can't legally terminate an employee's job:

- for refusing to commit an unlawful act, like lying to OSHA investigators about how an accident occurred in a restaurant kitchen;
- for performing a public obligation like serving on a jury or serving in a military reserve unit;
- for a discriminatory reason, such as that you learned your brewmaster is a transgender woman or that your catering manager is Muslim;
- as retaliation for making a claim against the employer, as when an African American tasting-room server files a charge with EEOC alleging race-based discrimination;
- for exercising a statutory right, like filing for workers' compensation after being burned by a fryer; or
- for whistleblowing (reporting a violation of law to government authorities), such as reporting a safety violation to the FDA or tax evasion to the IRS.

This is true even in at-will employment, so carefully document your reasons for all disciplinary actions and terminations.

CHAPTER 19

Keeping Taxes Low

A business in the food and beverage industry can enhance its profitability by increasing sales or by reducing expenses. While careful purchasing goes far in expense reduction, taxes profoundly affect profitability. As a result, prudent businesspeople determine the tax consequence of virtually every transaction, which means you should schedule periodic meetings with your business lawyer and tax accountant. At least one year-end planning session for the purpose of evaluating business activities and tax planning is advisable.

After allowing for basic needs through a standard deduction or certain specified deductions (personal exemptions were eliminated effective in 2018), the federal income tax system is essentially a fixed-rate system. There are now seven graduated tax rates for individuals (10, 12, 22, 24, 32, 35, and 37 percent) and a corporate rate of 21 percent. Two means of reducing tax liability are spreading taxable income and using tax deductions effectively. Spreading income often involves postponing payments that would otherwise be made and entails some risk. For example, the party owing the money might not be willing to pay interest or might go broke before the debt is fully paid.

INCOME SPREADING

Installments

One way a business can spread income is to receive payment in installments. With some exceptions, the Internal Revenue Code (IRC) allows a taxpayer who sells property with payments received in successive tax years to report the income on an installment basis in some situations if the sale is properly structured. Under this method, tax is imposed only as payments are received. Installment sales are generally not available for the sale of inventory, however.

Suppose you remodel your restaurant kitchen and sell your used equipment for $15,000. Ordinarily, the entire $15,000 would be taxable income in the year you received the funds (not allowing for recaptured depreciation, which is beyond the scope of this discussion). If, however, you use the installment method with three annual payments of $5,000, income from the sale is taxed as the installments are received. In either case, the amount of income is $15,000, but under the installment method, the amount is spread out over three years, and you might be able to take advantage of being in a lower tax bracket than had you taken the full $15,000 in the year you sold the equipment.

Be sure to check with your CPA about whether the installment method is right for your particular situation before you put your assets up for sale. Also, care must be taken with the mechanics of this arrangement. If a business sells a product for a negotiable note due in full at some future date or for some other deferred-payment obligation that's essentially equivalent to cash or that has an ascertainable fair market value, the business may have to report the total proceeds of the sale as income realized when the note is received, not when the note is paid off with cash. (A negotiable note is a written and signed promise to pay a specified sum of money either on demand or at a specified time, payable either to an identified party or to the bearer.) Be sure you discuss any planned installment sales with your tax advisor.

Deferred Payments

If you're currently in a high tax bracket, you might want to defer income until the future. For instance, a caterer might ask a customer to pay for the November wedding reception the following year. This would result in tax savings if the caterer accounts on a cash basis and if, when the deferred amounts are finally paid, the caterer is in a lower tax bracket. This type of deferral generally isn't available for accrual-basis taxpayers.

Again, you must ensure that the mechanics of the arrangement meet the legal requirements for deferring taxes. Otherwise, you can be taxed on income you haven't received. This is called "constructive receipt." The IRS will consider that you received income—even if you haven't—when the amount is due if you're aware that (a) the amount has been appropriated on the books of the person who owes the money and (b) that person is willing and able to pay. Again, consultation with your tax advisor is recommended.

Spreading Income Among Family Members

Another strategy for business owners in high tax brackets is to divert some income to family members in lower tax brackets.

1. Employing Family Members

You might spread income by hiring members of your immediate family as employees. Putting dependent children on the payroll can result in substantial tax savings because their salaries can be deducted as a business expense. If the business is unincorporated then you don't have to withhold or pay FICA (Social Security and Medicare) taxes on those wages if the employee is an unemancipated child under the age of eighteen. Payments for the services of children under the age of twenty-one who work for their parents, whether or not in a trade or business, also aren't subject to FUTA tax (federal unemployment tax).

However, payments for the services of children of any age who work for their parents are usually subject to income tax. Your child, stepchild, or grandchild can earn up to the amount of the standard deduction without any tax liability.

Some additional restrictions on such an arrangement are:

- The salary must be reasonable in relation to the child's age and the work performed;
- The work performed must be a necessary service to the business; and
- The work must actually be performed by the child.

See IRS Publication 15, Section 3, "Family Employees," for more information.

2. Family Partnerships

A second method of transferring income to members of your family is the creation of a family partnership. Each partner receives an equal share of the overall income unless the partnership agreement provides otherwise. The income is taxed once as individual income to each partner. If, for example, you're a parent who heads a family business, you can divert some of your income to your family members so it will be taxed to them according to their respective tax brackets.

The income received by children is likely to be taxed at significantly lower rates, resulting in more income reaching the family than if it had all been received by the parent, who is often in a higher tax bracket than the children. If, however, a child is under eighteen years old (or under the age of twenty-four if a full-time student) and receives unearned income from the partnership, any amount over $2,200 is taxed at a special rate under the so-called "Kiddie Tax" rules.

Although the IRS recognizes family partnerships, it may subject them to close scrutiny to ensure that the partnership isn't a sham. In addition, the IRS might forbid the shift in income, in accordance with the Internal Revenue Code section that deals with distribution of partners' shares and family partnerships. The same section provides that a person owning a capital interest (or ownership interest) in a family partnership is considered a partner for tax purposes even if the capital interest was a gift, so long as the gift is genuine and irrevocable.

3. Family Corporations and Limited Liability Companies

Some families have incorporated or created family-owned limited liability companies. If the IRS questions the motivation for the incorporation, the courts examine the intent of the family members. If the sole purpose of incorporating was tax avoidance, the scheme won't stand. If the IRS successfully contends that the business entity should be disregarded, the IRS can reallocate income from the corporation or LLC to the individual taxpayer. This will be done, for instance, if the corporation or LLC doesn't engage in substantial business activity, doesn't observe proper formalities, or if its separate status isn't otherwise adhered to by the owners.

A bona fide (genuine) corporation or limited liability company being taxed as a C corporation, however, might provide some tax advantages for a small-business owner. As employees, the owners can control their taxable income with limited salaries. Although the corporation or LLC must recognize income whenever a sale is made, the corporation or LLC can deduct the owner's salary as well as other business expenses.

Incorporating or creating an LLC shouldn't be done solely for tax reasons, though. Although C corps are now taxed at a flat rate of 21 percent at the federal level, there are legal and accounting expenses related to setting up and maintaining a corporation or LLC, and double taxation is also a concern for entities taxed as C corporations. Consult with your tax advisor to determine whether Ccorp status is right for your particular business.

4. S Corporations

Another alternative for a small enterprise is to organize as an S corporation. Income from an S corporation is taxed only once at the individual level. Although income from a partnership or from being self-employed is also taxed only once at the individual level, the tax rates associated with the incomes are different. In an S corporation, income passed through to the owners (shareholders) as dividends isn't subject to FICA taxes, although regular salary paid to an owner is subject to these taxes.

In fact, with S corps, you must be careful not to pay too low a salary to the working owners. Doing so might result in IRS scrutiny if the result is too little employment tax withheld on income because too much of that income was distributed to the owner in the form of dividends rather than as wages.

5. LLC Tax Election

The tax laws allow an LLC to elect to be taxed like a corporation or to be taxed as if the business were still run as a sole proprietorship (in states allowing one-person LLCs) or a partnership. If no election is made, the default tax treatment is that of a partnership if there's more than one member, or a sole proprietorship if there's only one member. Some states have a gross receipts tax for LLCs that may make an LLC a less attractive option in your state.

Taxes on Accumulated Earnings

If you incorporate to postpone a significant portion of income, the IRS might impose an accumulated-earnings tax. Accumulated earnings beyond $250,000 must be justified as reasonable for the needs of the business or be subject to a tax of 20 percent in addition to the regular corporate tax.

BUSINESS DEDUCTIONS

Another means of reducing tax liability involves making use of various tax deductions. For this, you must keep full and accurate records, along with receipts. Even if your business is home-based, as are many start-up businesses, you should have a separate checking account and a complete set of books for all the activities of your trade or business. A hobbyist isn't entitled to business deductions.

> **ARPA Grants Excluded from Income**
>
> The American Rescue Plan Act of 2021 (ARPA) authorized the Small Business Administration (SBA) to award revitalization grants to certain restaurants, food trucks, brewpubs, tasting rooms, and other places where patrons gather to be served food and drink. All such grants are excluded from income for tax purposes.

Hobby or Business?

Tax laws generally presume a person is engaged in a business or trade, as opposed to a hobby, if a net profit results from the activity in question during three out of the five consecutive years ending with the taxable year in question. For instance, if you make and sell jam, and you don't realize any profit from that activity for at least three of the last five years, the IRS may contend your jam-making is a hobby, and you'll have to prove profit motive (intent to make a profit) to claim business expenses.

The US Treasury regulations call for an objective standard on the profit-motive issue, so statements of the taxpayer as to intent won't suffice as proof. The regulations list the following nine factors to be used in determining profit motive:

1. the manner in which the taxpayer carries on the activity (e.g., effective business routines and bookkeeping procedures);
2. the expertise of the taxpayer or the taxpayer's advisors (e.g., study in an area, awards, prior publication, critical recognition, and membership in professional organizations);
3. the time and effort expended in carrying on the activity (e.g., at least several hours a day devoted to the activity, preferably on a regular basis);
4. an expectation that business assets will increase in value;
5. the success of the taxpayer in similar or related activities (e.g., past successes, even if prior to the relevant five-year period);
6. history of income or losses with respect to the activity (e.g., increases in receipts from year to year, unless losses vastly exceed receipts over a long period of time);

7. the amount of occasional profits, if any, that are earned;
8. financial status (wealth sufficient to support a hobby weighs against the profit motive); and
9. elements of personal pleasure or recreation (if significant traveling is involved and little work accomplished, the court may be suspicious of profit motive).

No single factor determines the results.

Many of the cases discussing this issue are about activities like breeding horses and collecting art, but the same rules apply to food and beverage related businesses. You're especially likely to encounter this problem if your business involves activities that people often do for fun, such as brewing beer or decorating children's birthday cakes.

Unfortunately, hobbyists currently have the worst of all worlds—they owe income tax on the revenue from selling their beer or cakes, but since 2018 (and until 2025), they aren't allowed to deduct any of the related expenses because those expenses are treated as personal itemized deductions. These personal itemized deductions used to be allowed (although for nonprofit hobby income, limited to the amount of income from the activity) subject to a floor of 2 percent of adjusted gross income (AGI), but they were eliminated by the Tax Cuts and Jobs Act of 2017 (TCJA), effective for tax years 2018 through 2025.

For these reasons, it's important to become established as a for-profit business as soon as possible. Once you've established yourself as engaged in a for-profit business, all your ordinary and necessary expenditures for that business are deductible business expenses. This includes wages, ingredients, equipment, workspace, professional magazines, travel for business purposes, and fees for legal and accounting services.

Deductions for the Use of Your Home

If you have a home-based office, consider the pros and cons of taking a home-office deduction carefully. This deduction allows you to deduct various home expenses against your net business income. Expenses that fall into this category include, but aren't limited to:

- mortgage interest;
- real estate taxes;

- home repairs/maintenance;
- rent;
- utilities;
- insurance;
- security system; and
- depreciation.

Indirect expenses are those that benefit both the business and the personal use portions of the home. The business portion of the expense is taken as a percentage of the total spent. The business-use percentage is determined by dividing the square footage of the home used for business purposes by the total square footage. Direct expenses are those that were made to improve only the business-use portion of the home. These amounts are allowed in full. This standard method of calculating the deduction has some calculation, allocation, and substantiation requirements that are complex and burdensome for a small-business owner, so a simplified method is now allowed.

For returns filed in or after 2014, you can use a simplified option for computing the home-office deduction. More information on the calculation is below. See your tax advisor to determine the best method to calculate the deduction in your particular situation.

1. Regular and Exclusive Use

For an area of your home to be considered used for business, it must be consistently used for business purposes only. Generally, an area is considered to be used for business if it's used regularly and exclusively for business purposes and is:

- your principal place of business;
- a place where you meet and deal with your customers in the normal course of business;
- a separate structure that's not attached to your home; or
- a separately identifiable space used to store inventory or product samples when your home is your business's only location (while this use must still be regular, it doesn't have to be exclusive).

No home-office deductions are allowed when employees rent their homes to their employers in their capacity as employees.

2. Tax Advantages

Previously, the primary tax advantage of the use of a home office came from a deduction for an allocable portion of repairs, utility bills, and depreciation. Otherwise, these wouldn't be deductible at all. Under the TCJA, though, mortgage interest has become a more important deduction since many taxpayers who used to itemize now use the higher standard deduction. That law also reduced the amount that can be deducted for real property taxes.

To determine the home-office deduction under the standard method, take the square footage of the space used for the business, divide it by the total square footage of the house, and multiply the resulting figure by your mortgage interest, property taxes, etc. Determining the amount of allowable depreciation is highly complex, and you should discuss it with your accountant or tax advisor. The simplified option can significantly reduce the burden of recordkeeping by allowing you to multiply a prescribed rate (five dollars, as of the date of this writing) by the allowable square footage of the office, up to a maximum of three hundred square feet, in lieu of calculating actual expenses.

The total amount that can be deducted for an office or storage place in the home is artificially limited—the home-office deduction can't be used to create a net loss. Any disallowed home-office expense can be carried forward indefinitely and deducted in future years against profits from the business.

3. Tax Disadvantages: Selling Your Home

With some restrictions, there's an exclusion of gain for tax purposes of up to $250,000 ($500,000 for joint filings) on the sale of your primary residence. If, however, you've taken the home-office deduction, you could owe capital gains tax on a portion of the sale. If you plan to sell your home any time soon, confer with an accountant or tax advisor, because this may mean it's inadvisable for you to take the home-office deduction.

In Plain English

Most small businesses can immediately deduct the cost of certain capital assets.

Other Business Expenses

As mentioned earlier, deductible business expenses include not only the workspace, but also all ordinary and necessary expenditures of the business. Current expenses (items with a useful life of less than one year) are fully deductible in the year incurred. Office supplies, website hosting, and paper napkins are all examples of current expenses.

The cost of equipment, such as an oven, fermenter, or delivery truck, all of which have useful lives of more than one year, is a capital expenditure and can't be fully deducted in the year of purchase. Instead, you have to depreciate, or allocate, the cost of any capital expenditure over the estimated useful life of that item. Although the actual useful life of equipment varies, the tax code sets out specific periods over which depreciation can be deducted.

In some cases, it might be difficult to decide whether an expense is a capital expenditure or a current expense. Repairs are one example. If you spend $500 repairing your delivery van, this expense may or may not constitute a capital expenditure. The test generally focuses on whether the amount spent restoring the vehicle adds to its value or substantially prolongs its useful life. Since the cost of replacing short-lived parts of a vehicle to keep it in efficient working condition doesn't substantially add to its useful life, the cost is a current cost and is deductible. The cost of rebuilding your van's engine, on the other hand, significantly extends its useful life, so this is a capital expenditure and must be depreciated.

The tax code also allows a taxpayer-friendly election to expense certain depreciable business assets, up to a specified limit per year. This amount is adjustable for inflation annually. In 2021, this limit was increased to $1,050,000 of certain assets that can be expensed for the year and need not be depreciated at all (though this begins to phase out when the cost of your qualifying Section 179 property placed in service in a year is more than a certain amount—$2,620,000 for 2021). Only certain types of assets are covered, and there are special rules for vehicles.

Travel Expenses

With certain restrictions, you can deduct 100 percent of some of your ordinary and necessary expenses, including travel and lodging, so long as your travel is solely for business purposes. Business meals and meals consumed while on a business trip are deductible up to 50 percent of the actual cost. If the trip primarily involves a personal vacation, you can deduct business-related expenses at the destination, but you can't deduct the transportation costs. If the trip is primarily for business, but part of the time is given to a personal vacation, you must indicate which expenses are for business and which for pleasure. This can be more complicated than it first appears, and the rules are different for certain foreign trips, so check with your accountant or tax advisor for details.

Keeping a paper or digital expense diary is your best line of defense with respect to business expenses incurred while traveling. Keep proof of all expenses, and record the time spent on business and (if any) personal activities. List the places visited and the business purposes of your activities. If applicable, keep track of your mileage. You must keep receipts for all expenses of seventy-five dollars or more—less-expensive items can be recorded in your expense diary. Remember, accurate, detailed, and contemporaneous record keeping is the first and best line of defense for tax preparation.

In Plain English

In the past, certain business-related entertainment expenses could be deducted, but the TCJA changed the law so that you can't deduct any expense related to activities considered to be entertainment, amusement, or recreation, even when those amounts are spent on or for current or potential clients.

Charitable Deductions

The law provides that an individual or business can donate either money or property to qualified charities and take a tax deduction for the donation. Since this area can be quite technical, consult with your tax advisor before making any charitable donations. If you have any questions about the legitimacy of a particular charity, contact your state attorney general's office or the local governmental agency that polices charitable solicitations in your area. The IRS also maintains a current list of all eligible tax-exempt organizations nationally and their specific exempt status (see www.irs.gov/charities-non-profits).

Health Insurance

If you're a sole proprietor, you may be eligible to deduct the cost of health insurance premiums paid on a health insurance policy covering medical care when you have a net profit for the year. The policy can cover you, your spouse, and dependents, as well as your nondependent children who are under the age of twenty-seven at the end of the applicable tax year. The same rules apply to partnerships and to LLCs taxed as sole proprietors or partnerships. Entities taxed as C corporations can, with some restrictions, deduct the cost of health insurance premiums without those benefits being taxable to the employees as wages, but the rules are more complex for entities taxed as S corporations. The cost of health insurance benefits must be included in the wages of all Scorp employees who own more than 2 percent of the entity.

In Plain English

If you don't know whether a particular expense is deductible, consult with a competent CPA or tax advisor. Consultation with qualified tax professionals is always advisable to ensure maximum benefits. The resulting tax savings usually mean the consultation quickly pays for itself.

SPECIAL RULES FOR TAXES ON TIPS

Tips received from customers by employees of a restaurant, brewpub, or the like are typically subject to withholding taxes. Any employees who receive cash tips of twenty dollars or more in a calendar month while working for you are required to report to you the total amount of their tips in writing by the tenth day of the following month. Cash tips include tips received directly from customers, tips from other employees under any tip-sharing arrangement, and charged tips (for instance, credit and debit card charges) that you distribute to employees.

Service charges added to a bill that the customer must pay (for example, a large-party service charge at a restaurant, a mandated delivery charge for pizza, or a bottle-service charge at a nightclub) don't count as tips, but as non-tip wages, which are subject to FICA taxes and federal income tax withholding.

You can have employees use IRS Form 4070 (Employee's Report of Tips to Employer) to report their tips to you or provide other means for your employees to report tips to you, such as a system for electronic tip reporting. You must use these reports to determine the amount of FICA and income taxes to withhold for the pay period on wages and reported tips. You're responsible for paying the employer's portion of FICA taxes. The IRS has implemented two programs to help employers in the food and beverage industry comply with the tip-reporting requirements.

- Tip Rate Determination Agreement (TRDA): In this program, the employer enters into an agreement with the IRS to report cash and charge tips to employees at a fixed percentage rate, and the IRS agrees to limit the circumstances under which it initiates tip examinations.
- Tip Reporting Alternative Commitment (TRAC): In this program, the employer agrees to encourage employees to properly report all of the tips they receive and to provide periodic education to its employees about tip-reporting requirements. In return, the IRS limits the circumstances under which it initiates tip examinations and also assists the employer with training and reporting policies.

You can claim a tax credit for FICA taxes paid on eligible tip income, though amounts needed to bring an employee's hourly rate up to the minimum wage don't qualify for a tax credit. Ask your accountant or tax advisor for more information.

CHAPTER 20

Renting Commercial Space

At some point in the life of your business, you'll probably need to evaluate the terms and conditions of a commercial lease. Commercial leases are subject to a lot more negotiation than residential leases, which are tightly regulated in most states. Because there are few laws protecting commercial tenants, you should consult an attorney with experience in negotiating commercial leases before signing one.

PREMISES

To begin with, the exact space to be rented should be spelled out in detail in the lease. Determine whether there's a difference between the leased space and the usable space. Tenants are often required to pay rent on commercial space measured from wall to wall (commonly referred to as a vanilla shell), even though the usable space might be significantly smaller after the area is built out. You'll want to make sure the lease covers parking for your staff and customers as well.

If your space is in a shopping center or office building and you share responsibility for common areas with other tenants, your responsibilities for the common areas should be described. The lease should spell out who is responsible for cleaning and maintaining common areas like restrooms, elevators, hallways, and courtyards as well as whether there are any hours they aren't available for use by your customers and staff.

COST

The rent might be a flat monthly fee, but more frequently there are other charges. Restaurants and retail stores usually pay a preset monthly rental plus a percentage of revenues. Many commercial leases are "triple net" or NNN. In these leases, a tenant is responsible for its pro rata share of real estate taxes, building insurance, and maintenance on the property in addition to rent and utilities. In most cases, you'll be paying your prorated share of "common area maintenance" or "CAM" costs as well. These cover the costs of maintaining, repairing, and cleaning areas shared by multiple tenants, such as restrooms, parking lots, and courtyards.

Be aware that most small businesses will be required to have one or more owners personally guarantee the lease, meaning they're accepting personal responsibility for payment of rent and compliance with other tenant obligations. To evaluate the cost of the space, you should compare it with other similar spaces in the same locale taking all charges into account. Don't be afraid to negotiate for more favorable terms.

TERM

Consider the period of the lease. If, for example, you're merely renting a booth at a trade show, food fair, or farmers' market, you're looking at a short-term lease. On the other hand, if you intend to rent for a year or more, it's a good idea to get an option to extend the lease, especially for brick-and-mortar businesses. If you move every year or two, some customers may feel you're unstable, and customers who buy on an irregular basis might not know where to find you after the lease period ends. Worse still, a customer may find a competitor in your old space. For this reason, try not to enter into any lease that allows the landlord to relocate your business to a different space.

Long-term leases are recordable in some states. Recording, where permitted, is generally accomplished by having the lease filed in the same office where a deed to the property would be filed. Check with a local real estate title company or real estate attorney for the particulars in your locale. You should determine whether you want your entire lease to be a matter of public record or whether you'd prefer to have only a summary of it available for others to see (this is less expensive too, since recording fees are usually charged by the page).

In Plain English

If you're in a position to record your lease, it's probably a good idea to do so. You'll then be entitled to receive notices related to the property.

RESTRICTIONS

It's essential for you to determine whether there are any restrictions on the particular activity you want to conduct on the leased premises. For example, the area may be zoned to prohibit businesses that serve alcohol or stay open past 9:00 p.m. Try to put the burden of obtaining any permits or variances on the landlord and, if you're responsible for them, the inability to obtain them should be grounds for you to terminate the lease without penalty.

Be sure the lease spells out any restrictions on signs on the premises. It's not uncommon, for instance, for historic-landmark laws to regulate signs on old buildings. Some zoning laws also prohibit certain types of signs, and landlords often set their own limits on signs and what can be placed in windows.

Make sure the lease's description of your "use" isn't too narrow. If, for example, your use is limited to "Mexican food," you might find yourself in hot water if you later begin serving burgers and chicken tenders on your children's menu. You'll also need to carefully review the lease to see if you're restricted from opening another location within a certain distance of the leased premises. This is a deal-breaker for many businesses. If possible, you'll want to negotiate an "exclusive" for your specific type of business in the same shopping mall—for instance, a clause that the landlord won't lease to any other pizza parlor.

A common restriction in leases for food and beverage related businesses is that they must maintain an A grade for health and safety; if they don't, they'll be in breach of the lease.

If you plan to use the leased premises both as your personal dwelling and for business, other problems might arise. Zoning laws frequently prohibit certain forms of commercial activities in areas that are zoned residential, so consult with your attorney before attempting to operate out of your home.

CONDITIONS

Try to have the lease conditional on you obtaining any licenses or permits you might not be able to apply for until you have the address, such as health permits and liquor licenses.

REMODELING

Extensive remodeling might be necessary before the space is suitable for your use. If this is the case, the lease must set out which of you is responsible for the costs of remodeling, who determines the contractors used, and who owns the tenant improvements. In addition, you'll need to find out whether you'll have to restore the premises to their original, pre-remodeled condition when the lease ends. This can be expensive and, in some instances, impossible.

AMERICANS WITH DISABILITIES ACT

The Americans with Disabilities Act of 1990 (ADA), which was discussed in the context of employment in Chapter 18, also covers places of public accommodation, which are required to be "reasonably accessible." Further, these places must make reasonable modifications to their normal policies and procedures. For example, if customers normally have to carry their own food to the table, you may have to have an employee carry the food for those whose disabilities prevent them from doing so themselves; if you normally prohibit animals, you'll have to make an exception for service animals.

What is a service animal?

The ADA, which is a federal law, defines a service animal as a dog that is individually trained to do work or perform one or more tasks for a person with a disability. The task(s) performed by the dog must be directly related to the person's disability. You are required by the ADA to allow these dogs on your premises even if you normally prohibit pets.

An animal whose function is to provide emotional support or comfort doesn't qualify as a service animal under the ADA, even if the patron has a doctor's note. Nor do animals other than dogs qualify.

However, some state and local governments have enacted laws that do allow people to bring emotional-support animals into public places and/or to use animals other than dogs as service animals, so you'll need to find out what the law is in your particular location.

Places of public accommodation must remove physical barriers to accessibility when it's readily achievable to do so. In the context of your lease, this might include removing deep pile carpet that can't be navigated by a wheelchair, replacing round doorknobs with levers, raising toilet seats, widening doors, adding braille signs, and installing ramps.

If you make alterations to a place of public accommodation, you must do so in a way that makes the altered area readily accessible to and usable by those with disabilities, to the maximum extent feasible. The ADA Accessibility Guidelines provide specific details for creating accessibility, such as the height of the bathroom sink from the floor and the amount of pressure required to open a door. When negotiating your lease, pay attention to who covers the cost of ADA compliance—will it be you or the landlord?

ENVIRONMENTAL LAWS

You need to determine whether any of the materials used in your business violate federal, state, or local rules with respect to hazardous materials. In addition, there can be hazardous materials cleanup problems resulting from prior uses of the space you're planning to rent. For example, while many restaurants, brewpubs, and similar businesses love having a space with garage doors to open during nice weather, a space previously used by an automotive repair business might require an expensive cleanup operation before you can operate a food or beverage business there. Other issues, like whether your building contains any asbestos, lead-based paint, or the like may exist. The lease must spell out who bears the costs of any environmental compliance.

UTILITIES

If you need any utility hookups that don't already exist—maybe natural gas for your kitchen appliances—the lease needs to say who bears the cost of adding them. Of course, even if the leased premises already have the necessary connections, you should question the landlord regarding the cost of these utilities and ask whether they're included in the rent or paid separately. In some locations, garbage pickup isn't a problem since it's one of the services provided by the municipality. In other areas, renters are often responsible for their own trash disposal. In commercial spaces, this can be quite expensive.

MAINTENANCE AND REPAIRS

Are you or the landlord responsible for repairs and maintenance? Customarily, the landlord is responsible for the exterior of the building, including making sure it doesn't leak during rainstorms and that it's properly ventilated. Notwithstanding this fact, it's important for you to make sure the lease deals with the question of responsibility if, for example, the building is damaged and some of your property is damaged or destroyed. The tenant is often responsible for some—even all—interior repairs. The lease should spell out who is responsible for what with specificity.

INSURANCE

If you have to take out insurance for the building, as well as its contents, your cost will greatly increase. The lease should say who is responsible for insuring the building. Similarly, you should find out whether or not it's your obligation to obtain liability insurance for injuries caused in portions of the building not under your control, like common hallways and stairwells. You should, of course, have your own liability policy for accidental injuries or accidents that occur on your leased premises. See Chapter 17 for a discussion of business insurance.

SECURITY

If you're renting space in a shopping center or office building, it's likely that the landlord is responsible for external security, although this isn't universally the case. If you're renting an entire building, it's customarily your responsibility to provide whatever security you want. Read the proposed lease carefully to see what it says about this issue. Also determine whether the lease permits you to install locks or alarm systems.

FORCE MAJEURE

As we mentioned in Chapter 6, the COVID-19 pandemic has underscored the importance of force majeure clauses in contracts, and commercial leases are no exception. These provisions excuse one or more of the parties from performing their contractual obligations when specified circumstances beyond their control arise that make their performance commercially impracticable, illegal, or impossible. One court found that Illinois' pandemic-related closure orders triggered a restaurant lease's force majeure clause, despite that clause explicitly stating that lack of money is not grounds for force majeure. The court held that the tenant would still need to pay a proportional amount of rent, though, given that the closure orders allowed it to offer takeout and delivery. Another court, however, held that a similar statement in a force majeure clause meant that Chuck E. Cheese had no right to reduced rent despite the restrictions. Given this, make sure that any lease you sign has the broadest force majeure clause you can negotiate.

WRITTEN DOCUMENT

Make sure every item agreed upon between you and the landlord is written in the lease or one of the exhibits to the lease. This is good idea for all contracts, but is particularly important when dealing with leases, since many state laws provide that a long-term lease is an interest in land and can be enforced only if in writing.

CHAPTER 21

Retirement Plans

One of the most important benefits for employees is the ability to participate in a retirement plan. A retirement plan is a written savings program designed to replace a portion of employment income upon retirement. If the plan meets specific rules and regulations, it's called a qualified plan.

Contributions to a qualified plan are generally tax deductible for the person or business making the investments. Income taxes on the investment earnings are typically delayed until benefits are paid to participants. In the case of a Roth 401(k) plan, however, employee contributions are made with after-tax income and the earnings are tax-free.

A qualified plan is one of the last remaining legal tax shelters available to highly compensated individuals and can be used to attract and retain key employees. There are plans available whether your business is a sole proprietorship, partnership, corporation, or LLC—though not all plans are available for all sizes of businesses. There are essentially two types of qualified plans—defined benefit and defined contribution—and some hybrids.

In Plain English

The main difference between a defined contribution plan and a defined benefit plan is who bears the risk of poor investment performance—or reaps the reward of high returns. In defined benefit plans, it's the employer; in defined contribution plans, it's the employee.

DEFINED BENEFIT PLANS

Defined benefit plans (also known as pension plans) provide a fixed, pre-established *benefit* for employees at retirement. The amount of the contributions required to fund that benefit is periodically determined by actuaries. These types of plans are now rare in the private sector. Advantages include:

- These types of plans provide employees with a predictable retirement income.
- Businesses can generally contribute (and deduct) more each year than in defined contribution plans, so substantial benefits can accrue within a short time.
- These plans can be used to promote certain business strategies by offering subsidized early retirement benefits.
- A defined benefit plan can be designed to drain excess funds and allocate them to retirement on behalf of the senior preferred participant (the principal owner).

Of course, there are disadvantages as well, including:

- The business must pay for an enrolled actuary to determine the funding levels and sign annual filings.
- A defined benefit plan is the most administratively complex and costly type of plan.
- An excise tax applies if the minimum contribution requirement isn't satisfied or if excess contributions are made to the plan.
- Benefits can't be retroactively decreased.

DEFINED CONTRIBUTION PLANS

In a defined contribution plan, the *contribution*, rather than the benefit, is defined. Contributions are usually either a discretionary amount or a percentage of the person's annual compensation.

Profit-Sharing Plans

If the income from your business varies significantly from year to year, a profit-sharing plan may be the most appropriate type of plan to offer your employees, because contributions aren't mandatory, and the amount of contributions can be determined at or after the end of the tax year, either by a vote of your business's management or by a formula designated in the plan's documents. You'll need to have a set formula for determining how contributions are divided, and this money goes into a separate account for each employee.

A common method for determining each participant's allocation in a profit-sharing plan is the comp-to-comp method. Under this method, the employer calculates the sum of all of its employees' compensation (the total comp). To determine each employee's allocation of the employer's contribution, you divide the employee's compensation by the total comp and multiply each employee's fraction by the amount of the employer contribution to get each employee's share of the employer contribution.

Advantages of profit-sharing plans include:

- There's no set amount that the law requires you to contribute.
- Your business doesn't need profits to make contributions to a profit-sharing plan.
- Any size business can set up a profit-sharing plan.

Disadvantages include:

- Administrative costs may be higher than under more basic arrangements (SEP or SIMPLE IRA plans).
- You have to ensure that benefits don't discriminate in favor of highly compensated employees.

401(k) Plans

A 401(k) plan allows employees to contribute a portion of their wages to their individual plan accounts. The underlying plan can be a profit-sharing, stock bonus, pre-ERISA money purchase pension, or a rural cooperative plan. Also, 401(k) plans can have an automatic enrollment feature allowing the employer to automatically deduct contributions from an employee's wages unless the employee makes an election not to contribute or to contribute a different amount.

Generally, employees' contributions reduce their income taxes in the year they're made, but withdrawals are taxed. With a Roth 401(k) plan, employees make contributions with post-tax income, but withdrawals are tax-free. Employer matching contributions are still made with pretax dollars and taxed on withdrawal. There are three basic types of 401(k) plans: the traditional 401(k), the safe harbor 401(k), and the automatic-enrollment 401(k).

Traditional 401(k) Plans

A traditional 401(k) plan allows eligible employees to make pretax elective deferrals through payroll deductions, and employers have the option of making contributions on behalf of all participants, making matching contributions based on employees' elective deferrals, or both. These employer contributions can be immediately vested or subject to a vesting schedule that makes an employee's right to employer contributions nonforfeitable only after a specified period of time.

Contributions made under the plan must meet specific nondiscrimination requirements, and employers are required to perform annual tests to verify that deferred wages and employer matching contributions don't discriminate in favor of highly compensated employees.

Safe Harbor 401(k) Plans

A safe harbor 401(k) plan is similar to a traditional 401(k) plan, but, among other differences, it must provide for employer contributions that are fully vested when made. These contributions may be limited to employees who contribute or made on behalf of all eligible employees, regardless of whether they contribute. The safe harbor 401(k) plan isn't subject to the annual nondiscrimination tests that apply to traditional 401(k) plans.

SIMPLE 401(k) Plans

The SIMPLE 401(k) gives small businesses a cost-efficient way to offer retirement benefits to their employees. As with a safe harbor 401(k) plan, the employer is required to make employer contributions that are fully vested. A SIMPLE 401(k) plan isn't subject to the annual nondiscrimination tests that apply to traditional 401(k) plans. This type of plan is available only to employers with one hundred or fewer employees who received at least $5,000 in compensation from the employer for the preceding calendar year.

IRA-Based Plans

An IRA is the most basic sort of retirement arrangement. Although people tend to think of an IRA as something just for individuals, employers can offer their employees retirement plans that help them set up and fund their IRAs.

Payroll Deduction IRA

Under a Payroll Deduction IRA, an employee establishes an IRA (either a Traditional or a Roth IRA) with a financial institution. The employee then authorizes a payroll deduction for the IRA. All the employer has to do is transmit the deduction authorized by the employee to the financial institution. In general, if this arrangement is offered to any employee it should be offered to all employees.

This is probably the simplest and least expensive retirement arrangement that a business can have. No plan document needs to be adopted under this arrangement, and the employer has no filing requirements. Any size business can provide this plan, and all contributions are made by employees. Because employers aren't contributing at all, employees are not likely to be happy with this plan. Employees might or might not be able to deduct their contributions, but employers can't take a deduction, because they aren't contributing anything.

SIMPLE IRAs

SIMPLE IRA plans allow employers and employees to set aside money in retirement accounts without the start-up and operating costs of a conventional retirement plan. For this reason, a SIMPLE IRA is one of the most commonly used retirement plans for small businesses with a small number of employees.

These plans are available to any small business (typically with one hundred or fewer employees), but the employer can't have any other retirement plans. Each year, the employer is required to contribute for each eligible employee either a matching contribution up to 3 percent of compensation (not limited by the annual compensation limit) or a 2 percent nonelective contribution. Employees are always 100 percent vested in all SIMPLE IRA funds.

Simplified Employee Pension (SEP) Plans

Like SIMPLE IRA plans, Simplified Employee Pension (SEP) plans allow employers and employees to set aside money in retirement accounts without the start-up and operating costs of a conventional retirement plan. The main difference between SEP plans and SIMPLE IRA plans is that only the employer contributes to a SEP plan. Again, the employer can't have any other plan, and employees are always 100 percent vested in all SEP-IRA money. Annual contributions are flexible, but the employer must contribute equally for all eligible employees.

Money Purchase Plans

With a money purchase plan, the employer is required to contribute to the plan each year. The plan states the contribution percentage that is required, and an excise tax applies if the minimum contribution requirement isn't satisfied. Money purchase plans used to have higher deductible limits than profit-sharing plans, but this is no longer the case. Administrative costs can be higher for these plans than under more basic arrangements, and employers must ensure that benefits don't discriminate in favor of highly compensated employees.

SARSEP Plans

A fourth type of IRA-Based plan is the SARSEP, but this plan can't be set up now. It must have been established before 1997.

EMPLOYEE STOCK OWNERSHIP PLANS (ESOPS)

An employee stock ownership plan (ESOP) is a qualified defined contribution plan that is either a stock bonus plan or a stock bonus/money purchase plan. An ESOP must be designed to invest primarily in qualifying employer securities. These plans must meet complex requirements and can be expensive to set up. ESOPs are not usually useful for owners of small businesses.

HYBRID PLANS

As of this writing, there is a proposal to create a so-called "composite plan" for multiemployer pension plans maintained as part of a collective bargaining agreement. The composite plan combines elements from both the defined contribution and defined benefit plans. Employers pay in at a fixed rate, and retirees receive benefits for life. Unlike a pension plan, the amount of benefits can vary.

The target-benefit plan is receiving renewed interest as a result of changes in income tax law. This hybrid plan combines the contribution and benefit levels of a defined contribution plan with the recognition for mature employees found in defined benefit plans. Another hybrid, the age-weighted profit-sharing plan (AWPSP), is also available. As with the target-benefit plan, the contributions are weighted or skewed toward senior employees.

DESIGNING AND DOCUMENTING A PLAN

Most qualified plans require the employer to create and adopt a written plan document and trust agreement before the end of the first plan year. A summary plan description must also be drafted to inform participants about the plan. Documentation is available in two forms—prototype documents and individually drafted documents. Each form has its own advantages and limitations.

Because of this, you'll need to work with an experienced professional when selecting and establishing a plan. Another reason to obtain professional assistance is that most retirement plans have complex rules that must be precisely followed with regard to many elements of those plans, including vesting, contributions, eligibility, and discrimination in favor of key employees.

INVESTMENTS IN A QUALIFIED PLAN

The primary governing law regarding investments made by a qualified plan comes from the Employee Retirement Income Security Act (ERISA). Under its Prudent Expert Investment Principle, investments should be made with primary consideration given to what an expert, rather than an amateur investor, would do. Confer with a registered investment advisor or certified financial planner to structure your plan investments based on the plan's goals, the economy, and other relevant factors.

Because penalties apply to early withdrawals from qualified plans as well as to situations where required minimum distributions (RMDs) aren't taken, it's important for employees to work with registered investment advisors or certified tax planners as well. RMD rules, which generally require you to begin withdrawing funds from your retirement account when you reach the age of 72 (70½ if you reached 70½ before January 1, 2020), apply to all employer-sponsored retirement plans.

CHAPTER 22

Estate Planning

No matter what business you're involved with and no matter how successful you are in that business, the time that you'll work with your business is limited by either retirement or death. Prudent businesspeople make appropriate plans for both. This is commonly known as succession planning. See Chapter 21 for more information about retirement plans. In this chapter, we discuss estate planning, which means thinking about what you want to happen to your business and other assets upon your death or incapacity and then creating the necessary legal documents.

Proper estate planning requires the assistance of a knowledgeable lawyer. In some cases, you may also need a life insurance agent, an accountant, a real estate agent, or a bank trust officer. What help you need depends on the nature and size of your estate. This chapter isn't a substitute for the aid of a lawyer experienced in estate planning. Rather, it's intended to introduce you to the basic concepts, alert you to potential problems, and help prepare you to work more efficiently with your lawyer and any other professionals you're working with. For more in-depth information, see *Estate Planning (in Plain English)®*, by Leonard D. DuBoff and Amanda Bryan.

THE WILL

A will is a legal instrument by which you direct the distribution of property that remains in your estate after your death. A person who executes a will is called the testator ("executing" means signing in accordance with legal requirements). Recipients of gifts are known as beneficiaries or legatees. Gifts given by a will are referred to as bequests (personal property) or devises (real estate). Certain formalities are required by state law to create a valid will. About half the states require a will to be in writing and signed by the testator in the presence of two or more witnesses. These are called formally witnessed wills. Other states allow holographic wills that don't have to be witnessed or notarized, though they do have to be entirely handwritten and signed by the testator.

A will is a unique document in a couple of respects. First, if properly drafted, it's ambulatory, meaning it can accommodate changes in circumstances occurring after the will is executed, such as property acquisitions and new grandchildren. Second, a will is revocable, meaning you can change or revoke it at any time. Even if you agree not to revoke your will, you can still do so, though you might be liable for breach of contract.

Courts don't usually consider a will to have been revoked unless the testator either performed a physical act of revocation, such as burning or tearing up a will with the intent to revoke it, or later executed a valid will that revoked the previous will. Most state statutes also provide for automatic revocation of a will, in whole or in part, if the testator gets divorced or married after the will is signed.

To change your will, you have to execute a supplement, known as a codicil, with the same formal requirements as those for creating a will. To the extent that a codicil contradicts a will, the contradicted parts of the will are revoked. Codicils were more often used in the days before computers, since retyping the entire will could be burdensome. Today, it's more common to execute a new will that incorporates the changes.

Advantages to Having a Will

A will allows you to decide how your property will be distributed after your death. You can even make those gifts conditional. If, for example, you want to donate your collection of antique brewing equipment to a beer museum, your will can make the donation conditional on the museum agreeing to display the collection and not merely keep it in storage.

In addition, a will permits you to give property to minors while controlling the timing and uses of the property given. You might, for instance, require that the funds be used exclusively for education. A will also lets you nominate an executor (or personal representative) to administer your estate in accordance with your wishes and the applicable law. If no executor is named in your will, the court will appoint one.

If you have unusual types of property like antiques, artwork, publishable manuscripts, or intellectual property, it's a good idea to appoint joint executors, one with financial expertise and the other with expertise in the type of property in question. If you name joint executors, your will should describe how any deadlock will be resolved. For example, a neutral third party might be appointed as an arbitrator who is directed to resolve any impasse after hearing both sides. It's also advisable to define the scope of the executor's power.

A lawyer's help is necessary to ensure your wishes are described in legally enforceable, unambiguous terms. You must avoid careless language that might be subject to attack by survivors unhappy with the will's provisions. A lawyer's assistance is also crucial to avoid making bequests that aren't legally enforceable because they're contrary to public policy. An example is a bequest conditioned on the beneficiary getting a divorce.

Payment of the Testator's Debts

When there isn't enough in a testator's estate to satisfy all the gifts in the will after debts and taxes have been paid, some or all of the bequests and devises have to be reduced or even eliminated. This process is known as abatement, and the method for reducing gifts is set by state law according to the category of each bequest or devise. The legally significant categories of gifts are generally as follows:

- specific bequests or devises, meaning gifts of identifiable items ("I give my sister Elizabeth all the furniture in my home");
- demonstrative bequests or devises, meaning gifts that are to be paid out of a specified source unless that source contains insufficient funds, in which case the gifts are paid out of the general assets ("I give my brother Matthew $1,000 to be paid from my shares of stock in ABC Corporation");
- general bequests, meaning gifts to be paid out of the general assets of an estate ("I give my friends John and Melissa each $1,000"); and
- residuary bequests or devises, meaning gifts of whatever is left in the estate after all other gifts and expenses are satisfied ("I give the rest, residue, and remainder of my estate to my children in equal shares").

Intestate property, which isn't covered by a will but is part of the testator's estate, is usually the first to be taken to satisfy claims against the estate, though if the will contains a valid residuary clause, there won't be any such property, since all of your assets are covered by the will. Next, residuary bequests are taken. If more money is needed, general bequests are taken, and, lastly, specific and demonstrative bequests are taken together in proportion to their value. Some states, however, provide that all gifts, regardless of type, abate proportionately.

Disposition of Property Not Willed

If you acquire more property after signing your will, the disposition of that property is usually still governed by your will. If it falls within the description of an existing category in the will, it passes along with all similar property. For instance, if you buy a vacation home after you sign your will and your will says, "I give all my real estate to my niece Jordan," the new vacation home goes to Jordan. If it doesn't fall into a category described in your will and your will has a valid residuary clause, the after-acquired property goes to the residuary beneficiaries. Otherwise, that property passes outside your will to the persons specified in your state's law of intestate succession.

INTESTATE SUCCESSION

When a person dies without leaving a valid will, this is known as dying intestate. The estate of a person who dies intestate is distributed according to the state laws of intestate succession, which specify who is entitled to what proportion of the estate. Typically, intestate property passes to those persons having the nearest degree of kinship to the decedent. An intestate person's surviving spouse always receives a share, usually at least one third of the estate.

Each of an intestate person's surviving children (whether biological or adopted) typically gets a share, and if a child has already passed away, their children may be entitled to a share by representation. Representation is a legal principle meaning that if an heir doesn't survive the testator but has one or more children who do, that child—or those children—represent the non-surviving heir and receive their parent's share in the estate. In other words, the surviving child stands in the shoes of a dead parent in order to inherit from a grandparent who dies intestate. For example, if your son Joshua predeceases you and has two children who survive you, each of them receives half of Joshua's share.

If there are no direct descendants surviving, the intestate person's surviving spouse either receives the entire estate or shares it with the intestate person's parents. If there's neither a surviving spouse nor any surviving direct descendants, the estate may be distributed to the person's parents or, if the parents haven't survived the decedent, to their siblings by representation. If there are no surviving persons in any of these categories, in most states, the estate goes to surviving grandparents and their direct descendants.

In this way, the family tree is constantly expanded in search of surviving relatives. The laws of intestate succession make no provision for friends or in-laws, and most states make no provision for stepchildren. If none of the persons specified in the law of intestate succession survive the testator, the intestate's property ultimately goes to the state. This is known as escheat—and is one reason that everyone should have a will.

ELECTIVE SHARE

State laws often provide a testator's surviving spouse with certain benefits from the estate even if the spouse is left out of the testator's will. These statutes give the surviving spouse the right to elect against the will. In most states, the surviving spouse's elective share is one third or one half. Some states also allow children to elect against the will.

ESTATE TAXES

In addition to giving you control over the distribution of your property after your death, a carefully drafted will can greatly reduce the overall amount of estate tax owed. Note that the following information relates only to federal estate taxation. Although state tax law often contains similar provisions, state law must always be consulted for specifics.

Gross Estate

The first step in evaluating an estate for tax purposes is determining the gross estate. Your gross estate includes all property you had significant control over at the time of your death. Examples include bank accounts, real estate, investments, life insurance proceeds, annuities, jointly held interests, and revocable transfers. Under current tax laws, the executor of an estate can choose to value the property in the estate either as of the date of death or as of the date six months after death.

The estate property has to be valued in its entirety at the time chosen, although if the executor chooses to value the estate six months after death and some property is distributed or sold before then, that property is valued as of the date of distribution or sale. Fair market value is defined as the price at which property would change hands between a willing buyer and a willing seller when both the buyer and seller have reasonable knowledge of all relevant facts. It's often difficult to make this determination, especially when items like a non-publicly traded business, artwork, or intellectual property are involved.

Although the initial determination of fair market value is usually made by the executor when the estate tax return is filed, the Internal Revenue Service (IRS) might disagree with the executor's valuation and assign assets a much higher fair market value (the IRS even has its own Art Advisory Panel that evaluates appraisals submitted by taxpayers in support of the fair market value claimed for works of art). When this happens, a court decides the matter. In most cases, the burden is on the taxpayer to prove the value of the asset, so expert testimony and evidence of the sale of the same or similar properties are helpful. Courts are usually reluctant to determine valuation by formula.

The Taxable Estate

Calculating the "taxable estate" is the second major step in evaluating an estate for tax purposes. A number of deductions are subtracted from the gross estate to determine the taxable estate. The amount of tax owed is based on the taxable estate. Typical deductions from the gross estate include funeral expenses, estate administration expenses, debts, enforceable claims against the estate, mortgages and liens, and perhaps most significant, marital and charitable deductions.

1. Marital Deduction

The marital deduction allows the total value of any interest in property that passes from the deceased person to the surviving spouse to be subtracted from the value of the gross estate, although different rules apply if your spouse isn't a US citizen. Ordinarily the government is paid tax on this property when the surviving spouse dies, but the spouse can use estate planning procedures to reduce or eliminate estate tax. The marital deduction can be taken even in the absence of a will making a gift to the surviving spouse, because, as discussed above, state law typically provides that the spouse is entitled to an elective share.

2. Charitable Deduction

A charitable deduction is allowed when the estate donates money or property to a qualified charity. Since the definition of a charity for tax purposes is quite technical, if you're concerned about estate taxes, it's a good idea to insert a clause in your will saying that if the institution you listed doesn't qualify for the charitable deduction, the bequest will instead go to a substitute qualified institution chosen by your executor.

3. Calculating and Paying the Tax

Once deductions are subtracted, the taxable estate is taxed at the rate specified by the Unified Estate and Gift Tax Schedule. The unified tax imposes the same rate of tax on gifts made by will as on gifts made during life. It's a progressive tax, meaning the percent paid in taxes increases with the amount of money involved. The rates rise significantly for larger estates. For example, the rate increases from 18 percent, when the cumulative total of taxable estate and taxable gifts is under $10,000, to 40 percent, when the cumulative total is over $1 million. Federal estate tax is also reduced by a state death tax credit or actual state death tax, whichever is less.

Tax credits result in an exclusion that is available to every estate. For 2021, this amount is $11.7 million. Since 2011, estates of decedents survived by a spouse can elect to pass any of the decedent's unused "unified credit" to the surviving spouse. Previously, couples often needed complex trusts to take maximum advantage of their unified credits. The portability election makes it much easier for a married couple to engage in tax planning. With the unified credit, the vast majority of estates escape federal estate taxes altogether. If tax is owed, it's due when the estate tax return is filed (within nine months of the date of death), although arrangements can be made to spread payments out over a number of years if necessary.

DISTRIBUTING PROPERTY OUTSIDE THE WILL

You can distribute your assets outside your will by making "inter vivos" gifts (which means they're given during your lifetime), either outright or by placing the property in an irrevocable trust before death.

In Plain English

An inter vivos gift might mean considerable tax savings for your heirs if your business becomes much more successful after the date you make a gift of stock (or other business ownership interest) in that business.

Advantages

One reason to make gifts of your property outside your will is that the gifted property escapes the delays and expense of probate, the court procedure by which a will is validated and administered. In many states, though, probate is a relatively simple and inexpensive process, and in those states, there are few benefits to avoiding probate. In the past, there were also significant tax advantages to making inter vivos gifts rather than making gifts by will, but this changed when the estate and gift tax rates were unified.

One remaining benefit to lifetime gifts is that if a gift appreciates in value between the time you make it and your death, the appreciated value isn't subject to estate tax. If the gift were instead made by will, the added value would be taxable, because the gift would be valued on the estate tax return as of date of death (or six months after).

The other advantage to making an inter vivos gift is the yearly exclusion. Each year, you can gift a certain amount per recipient without owing tax or using your unified credit. In 2021, that amount is $15,000. This means if you give $20,000 worth of gifts to your son in 2021, only $5,000 is potentially taxable (depending on the availability of your unified credit). A married couple can combine their gifts and claim a yearly exclusion of $30,000 per recipient, so you and your spouse could give $30,000 to your sister tax-free without using your unified credits.

In Plain English

The unified credit and annual gift tax exemptions are subject to change, so check with your accountant to determine the current figures when you plan gifts.

Three-Year Rule

Gifts made within three years of death used to be included in the gross estate on the theory that they were made in contemplation of death. Amendments to the tax laws have done away with the three-year rule for most purposes, but it still applies to gifts of life insurance and some other transfers where the decedent has retained some interest in the property (such as a life estate or right to income from the property) or has the right to take back the gift (for instance, gifts made through a revocable trust).

Gift Tax Returns

You must file a gift tax return for any year in which gifts you make to any one person exceed the annual exclusion. Although it isn't necessary to file a return when a gift to any one person amounts to less than the annual exclusion ($15,000 in 2021), if you're concerned that valuation of the gift might become an issue with the IRS, it's a good idea to file a return anyway. Filing the return starts the statute of limitations running. Once the statute of limitations period has expired, the IRS is barred from filing suit for unpaid taxes or for tax deficiencies because of higher government valuations of the gifts. There's no statute of limitations for fraudulent returns filed with the intent to evade tax, though.

To qualify as an inter vivos gift for tax purposes, a gift must be complete and final. Control is an important issue. If you retain the right to revoke a gift, the gift might be found to be "testamentary" rather than inter vivos, even if you never exercised your right to revoke. The gift must also be delivered. An actual, physical delivery is best when possible, but a symbolic delivery may suffice if there's strong evidence of the intent to make an irrevocable gift. An example of symbolic delivery is when the donor puts something in a safe and gives the intended recipient the only key.

In Plain English

Many states allow joint bank accounts with rights of survivorship to serve as valid will substitutes.

TRUSTS

Another common way to transfer property outside the will is to place the property in a trust created prior to death. A trust is a legal arrangement by which one person holds property for the benefit of someone else. The person holding the property is called a trustee. The trustee can be an individual or an institution, and in some situations, it's beneficial to have more than one trustee. Those for whose benefit the trust is held are called beneficiaries.

To create a valid trust, the giver (called a "trustor" or "settlor") must identify the trust property, make a declaration of intent to create the trust, transfer property to the trust, and name identifiable beneficiaries. If no trustee is named, a court will appoint one. The settlor can also be designated as trustee, in which case segregation of the trust property satisfies the delivery requirement. Trusts can be created by a will, but property in a testamentary trust is probated along with the rest of the will. To avoid probate, a settlor must create a valid inter vivos trust.

Inter Vivos Trusts

Generally, in order to qualify as an inter vivos trust, a valid interest in property has be transferred before the death of the creator of the trust. If the settlor fails to name a beneficiary for the trust or to deliver the property to the trustee before death, the trust will likely be deemed testamentary, in which case, the trust may be deemed invalid unless the formalities required for creating a will were complied with. A trust isn't considered testamentary simply because the settlor retains significant control over the trust (like the power to revoke or modify the trust), though the assets in such a trust will be counted as part of your gross estate for tax purposes.

In Plain English

It's not uncommon for executors to be forced to sell properties for less than their full value in order to pay taxes. This can be avoided by obtaining insurance policies, the proceeds of which can be set up in a trust.

Life Insurance Trusts

Life insurance trusts can be used for paying estate taxes. The proceeds won't be taxed if the life insurance trust is irrevocable and the beneficiary is someone other than the estate, such as a friend or relative either in an individual capacity or as a business. This is especially important for businesspeople since, without a life insurance trust, their survivors might be forced to sell estate assets for less than their real value in order to pay estate taxes.

PROBATE

Briefly described, probate is the legal process by which a decedent's estate is administered in a systematic and orderly manner and with finality. The laws that govern the probate process vary from state to state. Because one of the principal functions of probate administration is to provide a means to transfer ownership of a decedent's probate property, probate administration occurs without regard to whether the decedent dies testate or intestate. In the course of probate administration, the following occurs:

- a decedent's will (if there is one) is admitted to probate as the decedent's last will;
- someone (referred to as the "personal representative," "executor," or "administrator") is appointed by the court to take charge of the decedent's property and financial affairs;
- interested persons are notified of the commencement of probate administration;
- information concerning the decedent's estate is gathered;
- probate property is assembled and preserved;
- debts and taxes are determined, then paid or challenged;
- claims against the decedent's estate are paid or challenged;
- conflicting claims of entitlement to the decedent's property are disposed of; and
- at the conclusion of the process, all remaining estate property is distributed to the appropriate persons or entities.

While probate administration is pending, distributions of the deceased's property are suspended to allow creditors, claimants, devisees, and heirs the opportunity to protect their rights. Probate property consists of the decedent's solely owned property as of the date of death. Property jointly held by the decedent and another person with the right of survivorship (e.g., a home or bank account) passes to the survivor and isn't a part of the decedent's probate estate. Likewise, the proceeds of life insurance on the decedent's life aren't part of the probate estate unless the estate is the designated beneficiary. Finally, assets owned by a properly drafted inter vivos trust aren't probate property. Using these types of estate planning methods makes it possible for a wealthy individual to die leaving little or no probate property.

PREPARING FOR INCAPACITY

Advance directives and durable powers of attorney help ensure your wishes are met if you become unable to handle your own affairs. An advance directive is used to describe your desires with respect to tube feeding and other types of life support, as well as to appoint someone to make health-care decisions for you if you can't do it on your own. A durable power of attorney allows you to appoint someone to act for you in non–health-care situations when you're incapacitated. You might decide to appoint one person to make business decisions and another to handle your personal affairs. In a general power of attorney, your agent's authority typically includes the right to use your assets to pay your expenses, collect government benefits, file, and pay your taxes, and invest your money.

DIGITAL ASSETS

Don't forget to address the distribution of your digital assets. When thinking about whether we need an estate plan, many of us don't consider just how heavily we rely on online accounts to handle everything from banking and shopping to storing family photos and chatting with our friends. Unless you provide login information for these accounts, your executor, trustee, or attorney-in-fact may not have access to basic financial information needed for probate. In fact, your executor might not even be able to determine what all of your assets are.

Because of this, a number of states have passed laws allowing executors, trustees, and those with power of attorney to access online accounts so they can properly perform their fiduciary duties. You do, however, need to make sure that your will, trust, and power-of-attorney documents affirmatively state that you grant this authority. Otherwise, the online providers' terms of service agreements will control, and the provider might delete the account instead of allowing access. Be sure your executor, trustee, and attorney-in-fact have all the information they need to properly handle your assets.

CHAPTER 23

Finding a Lawyer and an Accountant

Many people in the food and beverage industry expect to seek the advice of a lawyer only occasionally, for counseling on important matters like the purchase of a building or a threatened lawsuit. If your business is small or undercapitalized, you're doubtless anxious to keep operating costs down and don't relish the idea of paying an attorney to get to know your business if you aren't involved in an immediate crisis.

If this is your idea of an attorney's role in your business, you need to reevaluate it. Most small businesses would operate more efficiently and more profitably in the long run if they had a relationship with a business attorney more like that between a family doctor and patient. An ongoing relationship that allows the attorney to get to know the business well enough to engage in preventive legal counseling and to assist in planning makes it possible to solve many problems before they occur.

An attorney experienced in business law can give you the information you need to protect yourself from the risks unique to your business. Poorly drafted contracts, for example, can result in financially devastating lawsuits. Violating applicable laws, even accidentally, can subject you not only to lawsuits, but also to criminal penalties. Each state has its own laws, so a competent local business attorney is your best source of information on many issues that will arise in the operation of your business. Many law firms have attorneys who are licensed in several jurisdictions, and others have relationships with attorneys in other locales.

In Plain English

Most legal problems cost more to solve or defend after they arise than it would have cost to prevent their occurrence in the first place. Litigation is notoriously inefficient and expensive. You don't want to sue or to be sued if you can help it.

FINDING A LAWYER

You want either a lawyer who specializes in business or a general practitioner who has many satisfied business clients. It's an added plus if the lawyer has experience in your specific industry. If you don't know any attorneys, ask other people in your particular line of business (e.g., restaurant, wine-tasting room, brewpub, caterer) if they know any good ones.

Finding a lawyer who's right for you may require that you shop around a bit. Most local and state bar associations have referral services. A good tip is to find out who's in the business law section of the state or local bar association or who has served on special bar committees dealing with law reform. You might also see if you can hire the author of any books or articles covering the type of law you're looking for expertise in.

It's a good idea to hire a specialist or law firm with a number of specialists rather than a general practitioner. While it's true you might pay more per hour for an expert, you won't have to pay for the attorney's learning time. Keep in mind that it's uncommon for a lawyer to specialize in business practice and also handle criminal matters, so if you're faced with a criminal prosecution for the death of an employee, for instance, you should look for an experienced criminal defense lawyer.

EVALUATING A LAWYER

The most common way to evaluate an attorney is by consulting the Internet. Most law firms have established websites, and a firm's website often includes extensive information about the firm, its practice areas, and its attorneys. Today lawyers are reviewed on a number of websites such as Yelp, Google, and Avvo, but you should treat these reviews just as you would other customer reviews on other sites (e.g., Amazon). Some reviews are fake and search results on some platforms may be based on payments by the firm being reviewed.

After you've obtained several recommendations for attorneys, you should talk with them for a short period of time to determine whether you'd be comfortable working with them. Don't be afraid to ask them about their background and experience. You can also check with your state bar association to verify an attorneys' license to practice law and determine whether a lawyer has been disciplined by the bar.

USING A LAWYER

One of the first items to discuss with your lawyer is the fee structure. You can request an estimate, but unless you enter into an agreement to the contrary with the attorney, the estimate is just that—an estimate, not a flat fee. Business lawyers usually charge by the hour, though you might be quoted a flat rate for a specific service, such as incorporation or a simple will.

If you haven't consulted with a lawyer recently, review your business structure, employment policies, and other legal issues with your attorney, even if you're not aware of any problems. Also contact your lawyer whenever you think there might be a legal issue. Your attorney can help you identify which questions require legal action or advice and which are business decisions. Lawyers typically deal only with legal issues, though they might help you to evaluate business problems as well.

Take the time to develop a good working relationship with your attorney—it may prove to be one of your more valuable business assets. The attorney-client relationship is such that you should feel comfortable when confiding in your attorney. Your lawyer won't disclose your confidential communications; in fact, a violation of this rule, depending on the circumstances, can be an ethical breach subjecting the attorney to professional sanctions.

FINDING AN ACCOUNTANT

You'll probably need the services of a competent accountant to aid with tax planning, periodic reports, and annual tax returns, as well as to help you avoid tax scams, which are, unfortunately, quite common. Finding an accountant compatible with your business is similar to finding an attorney. Ask around and learn which accountants are servicing businesses similar to yours. State professional accounting associations may also provide a referral service or point you to a directory of accountants in your area.

Once you have a list of suggestions, review the accounting firms' websites for information about their backgrounds and specialties. Check with your state's accountancy board to verify the accountants' licenses and whether disciplinary action has been taken against them. Read internet reviews on sites such as Yelp, Google, and Angi with a critical eye, remembering that not all reviews are honest and that some sites prioritize vendors who pay fees to join. Interview prospective accountants to determine whether you feel you can work with them and whether you feel their skills are compatible with your business needs. Like your attorney, your accountant can provide valuable assistance in planning for the future of your business.

APPENDIX

Industry Associations

This is only a sampling of associations for the food and beverage industry. Search online for "[your specialty] and association" to see if there's one for your particular type of business.

American Craft Spirits Association: www.americancraftspirits.org
American Society of Baking: www.asbe.org
American Sommelier: www.americansommelier.com
Association of Food Industries: www.afius.com
The Bread Bakers Guild of America: www.bbga.org
Brewers Association: www.brewersassociation.org
  Its state guild/association finder: www.brewersassociation.org/government-affairs/state-guilds
Independent Bakers Association: www.ibabaker.com
International Association of Culinary Professionals: www.iacp.com
International Dairy Deli Bakery Association: www.iddba.org
Master Brewers Association of the Americas: www.mbaa.com
National Association for Catering and Events: www.nace.net
National Coffee Association USA: www.ncausa.org
National Restaurant Association: www.restaurant.org
  Its state restaurant association finder: www.restaurant.org/about/nra-partners/state-restaurant-associations
Retail Bakers of America: www.retailbakersofamerica.org
Specialty Coffee Association: www.sca.coffee
Specialty Food Association: www.specialtyfood.com

Tea Association of the U.S.A.: www.teausa.com
Wine America / The National Association of American Wineries: www.wineamerica.org
Wine and Spirits Wholesalers of America: www.wswa.org

About the Authors

LEONARD D. DUBOFF

Leonard D. DuBoff, founder of the law firm The DuBoff Law Group, graduated magna cum laude from Hofstra University with a degree in engineering and summa cum laude from Brooklyn Law School, where he was the research editor of the *Brooklyn Law Review.* He was a professor of law for almost a quarter of a century, first teaching at Stanford Law School, then at Lewis & Clark Law School in Portland, Oregon. He also taught at the Hastings College of Civil Advocacy and lectured for the AAA of the Hague Academy of International Law.

He is the founder and past chairperson of the Art Law Section of the Association of American Law Schools; the founder and past president of the Oregon Volunteer Lawyers for the Arts; the former president of the Tigard, Tualatin, and Sherwood Arts Commission; past member of the board of the Oregon Committee for the Humanities; former Special Projects Coordinator for the National Endowment for the Arts; and a recipient of the Governor of Oregon's prestigious Arts Award in 1990. DuBoff has testified in Congress in support of many laws, including the Visual Artists Rights Act of 1990. In fact, he assisted in drafting that law as well. He is also responsible for drafting and testifying in support of numerous states' art laws.

DuBoff is a practicing attorney specializing in the fields of art law, business law, and hospitality law. DuBoff was on the task force that drafted the Oregon Corporation Code and Oregon Nonprofit Corporation Code and began work on the Oregon LLC statute. He has represented numerous prominent restaurants, caterers, gourmet food retailers, and wineries as well. His scholarly articles and books are frequently cited by courts and commentators. He is a prolific author of law review articles and other publications and has written numerous books on art law, business law, and other related subjects. For more information, see www.dubofflaw.com.

CHRISTY A. KING

Christy A. King is an attorney in Portland, Oregon, where she practices law with The DuBoff Law Group in the areas of intellectual property, business, and hospitality law. She is coauthor of the *Art Law Deskbook* and *Art Law in a Nutshell* as well as earlier books in the *(In Plain English)®* series, including the first edition of this book. She is editor of the client newsletter published by her firm and author and coauthor of numerous articles in the fields of intellectual property, art law, and business law. King graduated cum laude from Lewis & Clark Law School and from Louisiana State University with a bachelor of arts in journalism.

Index

G

H

S